**A Question of Answers
Volume II**

Primary Socialization, Language and Education
Edited by Basil Bernstein
University of London Institute of Education
Sociological Research Unit

I *Social Class, Language and Communication*
   Walter Brandis and Dorothy Henderson

II *A Linguistic Description and Computer Program*
    for Children's Speech
    Geoffrey J. Turner and Bernard A. Mohan

III *Talk Reform*
     D. M. and G. A. Gahagan

IV *Class, Codes and Control, Volume 1*
    Basil Bernstein

V *A Question of Answers (2 vols)*
   W. P. Robinson and S. J. Rackstraw

VI *Social Control and Socialization*
    Jennifer Cook

A Question of Answers

Volume II

W. P. Robinson &

Susan J. Rackstraw

Department of Psychology
University of Southampton

ROUTLEDGE & KEGAN PAUL

London and Boston

First published 1972
by Routledge and Kegan Paul Ltd
Broadway House,
68–74 Carter Lane,
London, EC4V 5EL
and 9 Park Street, Boston, Mass. 02108 U.S.A.

Printed in Great Britain by
Clarke, Doble & Brendon Ltd
Plymouth

ISBN 0 7100 7068 3

Contents

		page
	Introduction	vii
9	**Content validity of the taxonomic scheme**	**181**
	1 Rationale and limitations of analysis	181
	2 The development of a matrix	187
	3 The sixty-four dependent variables	189
	4 The order of discussion	197
10	**Content validity of the taxonomic scheme: empirical data**	**198**
	1 Relationships within and between modes of answer for 'non-why' and 'why' questions	198
	2 Formal and contextual features of 'non-why' answers	256
	3 The relationship between formal and contextual features and the selection of answer modes for 'non-why' and 'why' questions	265
11	**The taxonomic scheme: summary and conclusions**	**278**
	1 Introduction	278
	2 Evaluation of the scheme	280
	3 Construction of higher-order categories	287
	4 Conclusions and implications	289
	5 Applications of the taxonomy	291
	Appendix B Coding frame for answers to 'wh' questions	**293**
	Appendix C The questions asked of seven-year-old children	**341**
	References	343
	Index	347

Introduction

In Volume I we sought to expose the differences in the ways in which middle- and lower-working-class mothers and children answered 'wh' questions. Before differences could be ascertained it was necessary to generate an array of aspects of answers in which these might be found and it seemed absurd to perform that exercise without some prior examination of the nature of questions. With some theoretical premises and earlier empirical work as guidelines, we produced a fairly delicate set of categories and distinctions that we hoped would prove useful for the original goal of evaluating the relationship between Bernstein's idea of the lower working class being generally confined to a restricted code of language use and the verbal behaviour actually produced. The taxonomic scheme for answers to questions was in fact successful in highlighting differences between the lower working and middle class very much along the lines predicted.

To check the utility of a taxonomy against the criterion of differences in use by groups of subjects is only one type of validation and with a fairly heavy capital investment in the data analysed, we judged it sensible to check the validity of the scheme in another way, with the additional possibility of introducing changes in it.

The strategy was to examine the extent to which the use of the categories covaried across subjects, after first eliminating covariance that might be attributed to other known sources of variance such as social class, control and communication index, and intelligence-test scores.

The objectives and means used are set out in Chapter 9, while Chapter 10 contains the empirical results, which are evaluated in Chapter 11. The full coding frame is provided in Appendix B, while the rationale underlying it has already been provided in Chapters 2 and 3 of Volume I.

While the emphasis in Volume I was social psychological with sociological and psychological overtones, the concern here is mainly linguistic. At present the fashionable focus of linguistic inquiry is the process-centred generative models initiated by Chomsky (1965), by comparison with which an attempt to generate a descriptive framework for classifying and discussing questions and their answers is likely to be viewed as quaintly old-fashioned and remote. However these are not disjunctive alternatives. While it is legitimate and useful to inquire into what *can* (could) be done with language, it is also useful to know what *is* done.

While it is exciting and informative to devise systems which could explain *how* sentences may be generated, it is also informative to classify ways in which produced utterances are organized, in this instance the concern being with the classification of a subset of verbal behaviour referred to as 'answers'.

That the 'answers' are those of a sample of thirty-three boys and twenty-eight girls about seven years old differing in social class and other attributes imposes limitations upon the generality of the results found. While the fact that they answered only twenty-nine 'wh' questions (see Appendix C) is also a limitation, the intention was to sample the whole range of 'wh' questions available in the language. A full description of the children involved and the manner in which the data were collected is available in Chapter 7 of Volume I.

Chapter 9   Content validity of the taxonomic scheme

1   Rationale and limitations of analysis

(i) The aims and methods of linguistics

The objective of descriptive or structural linguistics is to give a formal description of a given language as it is used by the normal educated native speaker. Such a formal description involves at the grammatical level the application of a set of relatively few terms to an infinitely large number of verbal utterances. It means deciding upon a feasible way of breaking down phonic or graphic substance data into units which are in turn made up of other units of a different order and so on. If we approach the task from the opposite direction, we decide upon what can be designated basic elementary units and proceed to classify each according to how it fits together with others to make up what might be called a 'higher order' or more inclusive unit. Each unit except the elementary ones can be described in terms of the pattern of lower-order units which make it up, i.e. in terms of its structure. Each unit except the most inclusive ones can be described in terms of how it fits into the pattern of a more inclusive unit, i.e. in terms of its function. Each unit may further be described as the member of a defined set, from which it has been selected at the expense of other members of that set: Lexical items, formally designated as such, may be described according to the likelihood and manner of their occurrence in the environment of other given lexical items.

Transformational grammar, on the other hand, involves reducing to a minimum the procedural rules that the ideal speaker of a given language would have to know in order to generate all the grammatical sentences of a language.

The differences between the transformational and descriptive approaches could be seen in terms of the emphasis of the descriptive linguist on analysing static corpuses of completed utterances and that of the transformational generative grammarian on giving a formal description of the process of speech production.

The derivation of categories for the description of the substance of a language depends upon the accumulation of samples of the language which is to receive a description. The methods of acquiring linguistic data are the subject of some controversy. Chomsky's preference for relying upon the 'intuition' of the linguist who is also a speaker for selecting or creating only grammatical utterances has led to a charge of probable subjectivity from descriptive linguists. The latter prefer to rely upon corpuses of actually occurring speech and writing in combination with native speakers' judgments passed on samples of speech or writing in that language as to their 'acceptability' or 'non-acceptability'. They in turn are charged with the error of trusting the linguistically naïve speaker's slender understanding of his own language and with confounding the data with time-wasting and misleading 'nuisance' variables which are of no grammatical significance.

The descriptive linguist who derives a taxonomic scheme which satisfactorily describes his language data and from which he wishes to generalize to all verbal utterances in that language does not have to claim that his breakdown and classification of units reflects the way in which a native speaker encodes, decodes or comes to learn his language. Likewise, when the transformational grammarian formulates his most efficient set of rules for the generation of all possible grammatical utterances, he does not assume that people in fact use these rules when they speak, listen to, or learn grammatical sentences in their language. It is true that psychologists and social psychologists have sought, reasonably enough, to see how far such grammatical models do apply to the behavioural processes of decoding and encoding—and with some positive results.

Although we are not committed to the relative efficacy of one linguistic enterprise or another, we have made use of some categories of a descriptive linguistic theory, within a static question-answer situation, and have generated a scheme for analysing answers to questions. Thus we have based our scheme on a set of categories and scales which are derived from data consisting of a relatively small number of utterances in the language. Moreover, the subjects whose speech we are concerned with are seven-year-old children and are not a typical group of speakers from the linguist's point of view. We have superimposed our three aspects of appropriateness, completeness and presupposition over the divisions which were adopted from descriptive linguistics at the linguistically defined levels of grammar, lexis and context. We have further included what might be called a semantic component in our utilization of 'modes' which separate out different types of information. Modes are further subcategorized according to particular areas of interest, and there are a few extra categories of formal and informational interest. We hoped that the scheme would be useful in several ways. Earlier chapters have pointed to two sorts of validity in a behavioural setting. Their concern may be represented by the following questions:

(a) Does a differential use of categories of speech correspond to socially based differences?

(b) Do these differences in use correspond to those which may be inferred from Bernstein's theoretical framework?

Thus the categories of the analysis form a focal point through which it is attempted to relate relatively crude social differences to aspects of a theory which seeks to describe and explain the differential linguistic orientation associated probabilistically with those social differences. The type of validity to be examined in this and the next two chapters is a third one:

(c) Do the categories of analysis give stable patterns of co-occurrence and dissociation by user such as to suggest that (1) they represent real alternatives rather than arbitrary divisions, and (2) they allow us to make some sort of higher order statements about them?

This sort of validation is parallel to those phonological and graphological linguistic enterprises which seek to establish the co-occurrence or complementary distribution of units.

There are limitations upon the generalizations we shall be able to make on the basis of any conclusions we might come to. The 'users' of our categories are a small number of seven-year-old boys and girls, who do not represent the whole spectrum of language competence or social background among seven-year-olds, to name but two relevant dimensions. Moreover, children of that age may be somewhat unstable in their verbal behaviour, and the situation in which they gave speech was again a limited one. The answers are to a small range of possible questions, and we are uncertain about their representativeness.

In spite of these reservations, it could nevertheless be a fruitful and worthwhile enterprise to see what we can say about the suitability and the implications of the scheme when used for the analysis of answers to questions like these from children like these.

We have partialled out the variance due to social class, I.Q. and the other independent behavioural variable, the Control and Communication Index, so that our data should represent associations and dissociations between scoring categories independently of the social class, I.Q. or C.C.I. score of the user.

(ii) Reasons for a correlational analysis

Correlational analysis is a common statistical procedure for examining the total network of associations between a set of variables. From such a matrix we can learn what tends to occur in the presence of what and also what does not. We shall base our conclusions on elementary statements of the form, 'Subjects who tend to make use of (i.e. score relatively high on) category A tend also to make use of category B', or 'Categories X and Y tend not to occur together in the answering behaviour of subjects'. We must then proceed to examine why this should be so. At the lowest level of interpretation, a positive relationship between two variables tells us that they have something in common with each other; a negative relationship implies complementary distribution. Variables which do not have significant positive or negative relationships are seen either as more or less equiprobable alternatives or as unconnected variables. Further interpretation of correlations involves introducing relevant information about individual variables. There are two main sorts of information which we seek to derive from the correlational analysis: (*a*) that which is to do with the validation of categories within the present coding scheme, and (*b*) that which suggests further groupings of the categories we have into more inclusive ones.

(a) THE VALIDATION OF THE SCHEME

We may discover that there are overlaps between categories, so that, for instance, one mode might be a better representation of a single viewpoint if it loses one of its subcategories. Of course, such a solution can only be suggested for categories which are divided into subcategories and where these subcategories represent such basic divergent attributes. We may fail to find clear distinctions between scoring categories and yet not have sufficient information about constituent elements to know whether it would be feasible and more meaningful to exclude certain of them.

Conversely, it may be that two scoring categories mean something similar and that if they were put together as one variable they would be more likely to have significant relationships with other variables. Again, ignorance of constituent elements and their relationships may prevent us from making appropriate adjustments to the scheme.

Where two variables share a common label it may be possible to look for information which tells us something about the validity of the same label being applied to the two. Have they really anything in common? If they are very closely related, however, the distinction between them that causes them to be counted as two variables rather than one might be a false one. An example of the same label being given to different variables would be where the same mode title, 'cause', is applied to answers to physical and social questions or 'categorization' to physical and moral questions. Also 'incompleteness' is applied at the grammatical, lexical and contextual levels.

We can summarize the concern we have about the validity of the coding scheme in the form of three questions, none of which can definitely be answered. They represent three lines of attack:

(1) Are the present categories too inclusive?
(2) Are the present categories inclusive enough?
(3) Are the labels we ascribe appropriate or not?

We hope, not only to diagnose deficiencies in the present scheme, but also to suggest possible rearrangement of the scoring categories according to information we have available from the correlation matrix.

(b) FURTHER GROUPINGS OF CATEGORIES

The second area of interest is to do with a further grouping together of the various categories into more inclusive ones whose labels will be derived according to the content of the particular categories concerned. Certain groupings are predictable on a theoretical basis; others may throw fresh light on the nature of some of our categories. There may emerge clusters of categories which are quite at variance with logical and theoretical expectations. Such a finding would have to lead to a thorough raking through of the individual categories to see just what they do involve as ways of answering questions or as features of answers.

(iii) The limitations of a correlational analysis

We shall deal with the disadvantages associated with this method of analysis under two headings, (a) those which affect the matrix as a whole, i.e. general considerations, and (b) those which affect only a section of the variables, i.e. specific considerations.

(a) GENERAL LIMITATIONS

The calculation of product-moment coefficients theoretically presupposes that the variables employed are normally distributed on at least an equal-interval scale of measurement and that the expected relationships between them are linear. We cannot claim such characteristics for a large number of our variables, many of which tend to be binary rather than scaled measures. However, it has been reliably demonstrated that the product-moment correlation is a robust statistic and that its use with two-valued variables does not introduce significant distortion unless the distribution is more extreme than 75/25.

A second general limitation is that, in such a large matrix as we are using, a relatively large number of significant correlations may occur by chance. Hence, although we do take account of the correlations which we consider relevant at each stage of the investigation, it is not worthwhile to spend much time puzzling over the single odd correlation which does not seem to fit any explanation. Also we must be cautious over drawing too hasty conclusions on the basis of a few relationships.

(b) SPECIFIC LIMITATIONS

The specific limitations are associated with interpretations of particular sorts of relationships, which in turn are partly a function of the scale characteristics of our data mentioned above.

There will be some positive correlations which can be explained by the necessary relationship between two variables. This will obviously be true where we have variables which represent a summed score for a category as well as those which represent its subcategories. A summed score will be likely to correlate positively with at least one of its constituent subcategories. This will be the case for the categorization mode as applied to moral questions and for others too. We might also include under this heading those variables which are dependent upon others. For instance, lexical presupposition can only occur where there is less than maximal grammatical presupposition, so that a positive correlation between lexical presupposition and less than maximal grammatical presupposition should be intepreted in the light of this dependency relationship.

There is the opposite case to the part-whole situation, where, because of the way in which the task was presented and analysed, subjects who answer in one way cannot answer, or are very unlikely to answer, in another way as well. Where there is a very limited set of, say, two or three choices, such a situation may lead to negative correlations between the categories which are available for answering in. An example of this is where 'mode 1' and 'mode other than 1' may constitute virtually exclusive alternatives for answering Q.1.

Other considerations to bear in mind when we interpret relationships are those of the particular content of individual variables, the particular content of the questions they are associated with, and the features of the situation which might reasonably be thought relevant. The relevance of content and context will be discussed later (p. 204) with reference to the use of 'modes 3 reference to own age', in response to Q.11, 'When did you start at infant school?' Certain of the questions given in their context allowed for very little variation in answering. The very high proportion of children who gave the answer 'With money' to Q.7, 'How do you buy sweets?' made a mode analysis futile. Other answers allowed a great variety. We cannot know the number and type of all predisposing factors which influenced the answers to these questions. All we can do is try to understand what each variable means in the context in which it occurs. To make use of the data obtained from the correlation matrix, we have to commit ourselves, albeit tentatively, to certain interpretations, having a proper caution against generalizing too far beyond the limits described by sample material and situational characteristics. The general procedure for interpretation is to impose certain divisions on the data, according to our present purposes, and to note patterns of relationships within manageable submatrices, We then ask about the patterns which emerge, 'Is there some obvious explanation or "story" which would explain these relationships?' If so, we have a closer look at relevant relationships amongst the variables, perhaps check against other correlations not in that submatrix and see if the 'story' still holds up. If it does not, we may look for another explanation. Within the confines of this analysis appeals to the validity of the story rely entirely upon internal consistency. While we may occasionally make use of knowledge of mean scores on variables, no external information is brought to bear.

2   The development of a matrix

The final scheme for the analysis of answers to questions post-dated the actual analyses. We were operating with intermediate versions at the time of the raw-data analysis.

Two sets of variables were derived, separated on the basis of whether they referred to the analysis of 'why' or 'non-why' questions. They also contained a certain amount of overlap which was built in with a view to reducing the two to one set or 'card'. Two correlational analyses were obtained for these two sets of data. The third and final correlation matrix took note of the correlation data relevant to the first two.

The data which were put on to the first two 'cards' were different from that which we have at present in the following ways:

(1) There were in all, more categories.
(2) There were some different categories (since certain were collapsed together for the third card, to save space).
(3) The scores for 'why' questions were for the first response only.
(4) The scores for Moral 'why' questions were based on the old rather than the revised coding frame (see p. 312)

The final card only allowed space for 64 dependent variables, after the necessary independent variables had been included. This is one reason why some variables were collapsed and others excluded altogether. Such rearrangements generally took place on one or more of the following bases:

(1) Two variables which were associated together logically or theoretically might be collapsed into one.
(2) Two variables associating together strongly in the matrix might be collapsed into one.
(3) Variables which differentiated subjects according to behavioural variables should be included if possible.
(4) Variables which were representative of major theoretical premisses should be included.
(5) Variables should have 'sufficient' incidence of occurrence and a 'sufficiently large' standard deviation.

The final card consisted of 64 categories used in scoring both 'why' and 'non-why' questions. The effects of I.Q., social class and C.C.I. were partialled out. Separate matrices were obtained for boys and girls, while there was also one for the total sample. When we refer to correlation data, we shall only use that from the total sample if it sheds further helpful light on what we have obtained for boys and girls separately. The effect of sex was not partialled out of the total sample matrix.

We shall be applying two tests of significance to the correlational data. One of these simply tests whether two variables have a correlation coefficient either positive or negative which is significantly different from zero. The second one tests whether two variables are significantly different from one another in their correlations with a third. Occasionally mean scores of various sub-groups or the total sample of subjects are used for evaluative purposes. In the first case we shall note relationships with 10 per cent or smaller probabilities of occurring by chance, while in the second all significant differences noted will be at less than the 5 per cent probability level.

3   The sixty-four dependent variables

We supply here a list of all the dependent variables of the matrix. Some of the titles will be different from those which are given in the various coding frames of Appendix B or in Chapters 2 or 3, where the coding scheme is outlined. Where titles do differ from those given in the coding frames, we shall normally supply the original titles as well, together with relevant reference numbers and letters, which should enable easy consultation of the appropriate coding frame. Although the titles may differ in this list, this does not mean that earlier headings will not be used to describe the categories we discuss where they are still applicable. They will rather constitute alternative ways of referring to the same category. The titles of this present list tend to be relatively brief, and this is because relatively long titles make discussion cumbersome. Thus the introductory sequence 'appeal to . . .' used in some mode titles will be dropped. A brief description is given of each coding category, while the place of reference for giving further information will also be made clear.

(i) Inappropriateness, incompleteness and presupposition in answers to 'non-why' questions only

A fuller description of these features is given in 'The Coding Frame for Inappropriateness, Incompleteness, Presupposition, Substitution and Other Miscellaneous Non-mode Categories' in Appendix B. Under each italicized title we give the original heading for each category as used in that coding frame. Following the brief description of criteria for inclusion in the category and in brackets, we describe each category in terms of the scheme which is presented in Chapters 2 and 3.

The relevant questions			Title		Brief description of criteria
Type	No.	Aspect		Level	for inclusion in categories
All	All	*Inappropriateness* Inappropriateness	*Grammatical* 1 Grammatically inappropriate answers		A minimal structural or systemic requirement not met (grammatical inappropriateness in the core area)
All	All	*Inappropriateness* Inappropriateness 5	*Lexical* Lexical inap-		A minimal lexical requirement not met or some other

B

The relevant questions Type	No.	Aspect	Title	Level	Brief description of criteria for inclusion in categories
				propriateness	vocabulary mistake made (lexical inappropriateness in all three areas)
All	All	*Inappropriateness* Inappropriateness 6		*Contextual* Contextual inappropriateness	An untrue item of information given (contextual inappropriateness in all three areas)
All	All	*Mistakes* Inappropriateness 2 +Inappropriateness 3 +Inappropriateness 4		*Grammatical* Question-answer discord Intra-answer discord Grammatical mistakes	A non-minimal structural or systemic requirement not met (grammatical inappropriateness in the concordant and residual areas)
All	All	*Incompleteness* Incompleteness 1 +Incompleteness 2 +Incompleteness 3		*Grammatical* Structurally incomplete adjunct Structurally Incomplete Nominal Group Other grammatical incompleteness	Some part of structure is missing from a unit (grammatical incompleteness in all three areas)
All	All	*Incompleteness* Incompleteness 7		*Lexical* Other lexical incompleteness	A relatively uninformative lexical item or a vague expression like 'sort of thing' 'and that' (lexical incompleteness in the core and residual areas except for uses of 'thing', substitute verb, and vague use of pronoun)
Where From + How	28 15	*Completeness* Information units		*Contextual*	An item referring to action, part, process, place (contextual completeness in the core area)
All	All	*Vagueness* Incompleteness 4		*Lexical* Vague nominal Group head	A relatively vague use of 'thing' 'do' 'get' or a pronoun (a specific type of lexical incompleteness in

| The relevant questions | | Title | | Brief description of criteria |
Type	No.	Aspect	Level	for inclusion in categories
		+Incompleteness 5	Vague pronouns	the core and residual areas)
		+Incompleteness 6	Vague substitute Verbs	
All	All	*Less than Maximal Presupposition* Presupposition 1	*Grammatical* Grammatical presupposition (*a*) Minimal +(*b*) intermediate	The first sentence of an answer does not simply consist of the minimal replacement group
All	All	*Presupposition* Presupposition 2	*Lexical* Lexical presupposition	A general substitute form is used in the answer to replace a more specific word in the question, e.g. pronouns for noun, 'do' for verb

(ii) Other non-mode features of answers to 'non-why' questions

Again the relevant coding frame for a fuller description of these features is 'The coding Frame for Inappropriateness, Incompleteness, Presupposition and Substitution and Other Miscellaneous Non-mode Categories', in Appendix B. However, not all these features are mentioned there, as their method of application is self-evident. Where they are mentioned, the earlier title will be given beneath their present one.

| The relevant questions | | | | Brief description of criteria |
Type	No.	Title		for inclusion in categories
How well How tall	8 22	*Substitution* Substitution 1	*Grammatical* Grammatical substitution	The grammatical form of a question changed in the answer to a semantically equivalent one.
All	All	*Substitution* Substitution 2	*Lexical* Lexical substitution	A word in a question changed in the answer

The relevant questions Type	No.	Title	Brief description of criteria for inclusion in categories
Where	2	*Misuse of preposition 'up' and 'down'*	'Up' or 'down' used where no indication of different levels
	4	(same title)	
	6		
Where	2	*Use of preposition 'round'*	Any instance of 'round'
	4		
	6		
Where	2	*Absence of proper name of place*	No map-reference or shop-name given in an answer
	4		
	6		
Where	6	*Name of sweet-shop*	An answer contains the name of a sweet-shop either alone or in a larger context

(iii) Modes of answer for 'non-why' questions

The relevant sections for fuller information about most modes of answer for 'non-why' questions are 'Coding Frame for Modes of "non-why" Questions' in Appendix B and also Chapter 3. It seems unnecessary to give the alternative ways of referring to these modes, since for answers to 'where' and 'when' questions their numbers correspond in all sections and for answers to 'who' questions there are only two modes. The 'functional definition' as a feature of an answer for Q.10 is mentioned in 'The Coding Frame for Inappropriateness, Incompleteness, Presupposition, Substitution and Other Miscellaneous Non-Mode Categories' under 'Functional Definitions for Type C Questions 2 Question 10'. It was later decided that it might be more appropriately considered a mode.

The relevant questions Type	No.	Title	Brief description of criteria for inclusion in categories
When	1	*Mode 1 objective*	Clock time or less precise but universal reference, e.g. 'four o'clock', 'In the afternoon'
When	1	*Mode other than 1*	Generally, time related to other events, e.g. 'when the bell goes'

The relevant questions			
Type	No.	Title	Brief description of criteria for inclusion in categories
When	11	*Mode 3 relative to own age*	One's own age given as reference point, e.g. 'when I was five'
When	11	*Mode other than 3*	Objective time reference or one relative to something other than own age given, e.g. 'in 1965', 'when my sister was a baby'
When	18	*Mode 1a: precise*	Exact date given, e.g. 'May 8th'
When	18	*Mode other than 1*	No date (not even month) given, but time relative to other event, e.g. 'in the summer holidays'
Where	2	*Mode 1 objective*	Street or town reference given, e.g. '69 Blank Avenue', 'in London'
Where	4	*Mode 1 objective or relative to Mode 1 for Q.2* (abbreviated to mode 1 +)	Either as above for Q.2. or related to a street or town reference given for Q.2, e.g. 'next door to me'
Where	6	*Mode 1 objective or relative to mode 1 for Q.2* (abbreviated to mode 1 +)	As above for Q.4
Who	9	*Unique person specification*	Teacher's name given, e.g. 'Miss Shark'
What	10	*Functional definition*	Mention made of what a school is for, e.g. 'learning things'

(iv) Modes of answer and their subcategories for why questions

A set of modes of answer for 'why' questions is given in Chapter 3. The two coding frames which explicate, subdivide and add to these are 'Coding Frame for Answers to All Types of "Why" Questions' and 'A Revised Coding Frame for Total Answers to Moral "Why" Questions'. Where the coding frames differ from the present list in their way of referring to modes and subcategories, the original titles will be given as well. Where the question content is moral, it is the different title according to the revised frame (R.F.) that will be given. Otherwise the original frame (O.F.) for all content types will be referred to.

The relevant questions Content type	No.	*Title* Mode and subcategory	*Brief description of criteria for inclusion in categories*
All	All	*Restatement* Restatement of Question as Answer (O.F.)	Repetition of question or of probe or of earlier response
Physical	23	*Regularity: alone* Appeal to Regularity (O.F.)	Some mention of frequency of the event of question or some mention of a season is the only information given in first response
Physical	23	*Regularity: qualified* Appeal to Regularity (O.F.)	Same as above (for 'alone') but as part of larger first response containing other mode(s)
Total	All	*Regularity* Appeal to regularity (O.F.) Appeal to regularity (R.F.)	Either mention of frequency or season for physical questions or invoking of tradition or normality for other content-type questions
Moral	All	*Authority: specified* Appeal to authority (R.F.)	Some specific authority is given
Moral	All	*Authority: unspecified* Appeal to authority (R.F.)	Basis of implied authority not made explicit
Moral	All	*Emotions: positive*	Feelings or wants given as reason in sentence in positive polarity
Moral	All	*Emotions: negative* Appeal to emotions, wishes (R.F.)	Same as above (for 'positive'), but in sentence in negative polarity
Physical	All	*Categorization*	Either the action or some participant or aspect categorized
Moral	All	*Categorization: simple* Appeal to categorization (b) general moral Appeal (A.B.C. orientations) (R.F.)	General moral judgment by terms like 'naughty' 'good'

The relevant questions Content type	No.	Title Mode and subcategory	Brief description of criteria for inclusion in categories
Moral	All	*Categorization: object* Appeal to categorization: All D. object-oriented (R.F.)	Property rights or possible value invoked
Moral	All	*Categorization: action* Appeal to categorization: All B. action-oriented (R.F.)	The action categorized, e.g. 'it is naughty' 'it is unkind'
Moral	All	*Categorization: person* Appeal to categorization: All A. actor-oriented + all C. other-oriented (R.F.)	Relevant person categorized, e.g. 'they're only babies', 'you'll be naughty then'
Moral	All	*Categorization* Appeal to categorization (R.F.)	Action person- or object-categorized
Total	All	*Categorization*	Action person- object- or aspect-categorized
Physical +Social	All Both	*Cause*	Event or state prior in time to event in question cited as reason
Social	13	*Cause: proximal*	Generally a specific disorder mentioned
Social	13	*Cause: distal*	Environmental feature mentioned as responsible
Physical	All	*Cause*	Inclusion in one of the above three categories
Physical	All	*Consequence*	Event or state subsequent in time to event in question cited as reason
Moral	All	*Consequence: positive* Appeal to consequence (R.F.)	Rewarding consequence mentioned
Moral	All	*Consequence: negative, actor-oriented punishment* Appeal to consequence: 2.A. (i) (*a*) + (*b*) (R.F.)	Punishment to actor following action mentioned
Moral	All	*Consequence: negative actor-oriented other ill-effect* Appeal to consequence: 2.A. (ii) (*a*) + (*b*) (R.F.)	Actor said to suffer after action in some way other than by punishment

The relevant questions Content type	No.	Title Mode and subcategory	Brief description of criteria for inclusion in categories
Moral	All	*Consequence: action-oriented* Appeal to consequence: B. General/action-oriented (1. positive + 2. negative)	A more general outcome envisaged, e.g. 'it may start a fight'
Moral	All	*Consequence: other-oriented* Appeal to consequence: C. other-oriented (1. positive + 2. negative (*a*) + (*b*))	Effect on person(s) other than actor mentioned
Moral	All	*Consequence: all negative general* Appeal to consequence: 2.A. (*a*) (i) + (ii) negative actor-oriented, general. + 2B. Negative general/action-oriented + 2 C (a) negative other-oriented general.	A general as opposed to specific undesirable result, e.g. 'you will be punished', but *not* 'you will be smacked'
Moral	All	*Consequence: all actor-oriented* Appeal to consequence: 1. A. positive actor-oriented + 2A. (i) + (ii) Negative actor-oriented	Any effect upon actor
Social	Both	*Consequence*	Event or state subsequent in time to event in question cited as reason
Total	All	*Consequence*	Inclusion in total of another or content type
Moral	All	*Emotions + consequence: other-oriented* Appeal to emotions, wishes: Other-oriented (i)+(ii) (R.F.) +appeal to consequence: 1.C. positive other-oriented + 2.C. (*a*)+(*b*) other-oriented. (R.F.)	A mention of wants of or effects upon person(s) other than actor as affecting action

(v) Other scoring category for answers to why questions

There is only one other scoring category for answers to 'why' questions. More information relevant to it will be found in 'Coding Frame for Answers to All Types of "Why" Questions'.

The relevant questions Content type	No.	Title	Brief description of criteria for inclusion in category
Physical	All	*Irrelevance* Additional Categories with Examples 3. Irrelevant items, but only where such an item is all that is given	A whole answer to a question is virtually unconnected with the content of the question

(vi) Refusal responses to 'why' and 'non-why' questions

A description of what these categories mean is found in 'A Revised Coding Frame for Total Answers to Moral "Why" Questions', Section II: the Problems, (*d*) Information.

Title	Brief description of criteria for inclusion in category
D.K., Don't know	An explicit refusal to answer usually of the form 'I don't know'
N.A., No answer	No explicit refusal is made, but the child does not answer

4   The order of discussion

In the next chapter we shall make our examination of categories in sections, depending first of all on whether it is mode or non-mode features which are being discussed. Within the sections defined in this way, we shall further separate, according to whether we are dealing with answers to 'non-why' or 'why' questions. Thus under the expressive heading, 'Relationships within and beween modes of answer for "non-why" and "why" questions', we shall discuss modes of answer for 'non-why' questions, modes of answer for 'why' questions, and modes of answer for both 'non-why' and 'why' questions, in that order. The features of form and context were scored only for answers to 'non-why' questions, but when these features are related to modes of answer, we follow the same order, 'non-why', 'why' and 'non-why' and 'why' together. A final separation is sometimes present, according to whether the discussion concerns the validity of categories in the scheme for analysis of whether it seeks to establish bases for the further grouping together of categories.

Chapter 10 Content validity of the taxonomic scheme: empirical data

1 Relationships within and between modes of answer for 'non-why' and 'why' questions

(i) Introduction

(a) WHICH ANSWERS WERE SCORED FOR MODE

Whereas all the answers to 'why' questions were coded for mode of answer, not all those to 'non-why' questions were. 'When' and 'where' questions had modes differing according to how relative the information was. 'Who' modes differed as to whether 'unique person' or 'role' specifications were given. The 'how' questions might have been divided according to whether 'principle' or 'process' were given, but such a separation was not entered into the matrix. A further mode variation concerned whether or not a 'functional definition of a school' is given in answer to Q.10, 'What is a school?' This mode was included, although it was never settled what other possible alternative modes could be.

(b) THE EXCLUSIVENESS OF MODES

The 'non-why' questions were usually interpreted as requiring a single mode of answer. The presence of more than one mode is very rare. Hence an examination of mode completeness (see p. 37) would produce little variance. This is partly a function of our having ascribed relatively few modes of answer to 'non-why' questions. The greatest number, four was originally applied to the 'when' questions. In contrast, 'why' questions offered at least ten modes, some of which had subcategories and, in giving an explanation, more than one mode was frequently used. However, there is a certain amount of mutual exclusiveness, such that, for example, a restatement is unlikely to occur with a causal explanation in the same answer.

(c) PROBING

The answers to 'non-why' questions were not probed, while those to 'why' questions were. This means three things:

1 There is an even greater possibility for a greater range of modes for each 'why' question than there is for each 'non-why' question.
2 There is greater 'unknown' experimenter-intervention for 'why' questions than for 'non-why' questions.
3 Whereas for 'non-why' we know exactly what question each mode is being used to answer, modes used in answering 'why' questions may vary as a result of the varying and unknown content given in the probes and intermediate answers.

(d) THE METHODS OF SEPARATING THE QUESTIONS

The answers to 'non-why' questions are separated by question, so that we relate the modes used to answer any one question to modes used for answering other individual questions.

The 'why' questions are partly grouped by content and only occasionally scored individually. Thus we have 'physical' questions, 'moral' questions, 'social' questions, but also a subcategory of 'distal' versus 'proximal' cause for Q.13, and the use of the 'regularity' mode is scored separately for the first response to Q.23, and subcategorized as to whether its use occurred alone or with other modes.

(e) HOW THE MODES ARE APPLIED

For answers to 'non-why' questions, the modes differ according to question type, although modes of answer to 'where' and 'when' questions are given similar labels. For answers to 'who' questions only one mode is noted, 'unique person'. For answers to 'What is a school?' one mode is scored.

Basically, the same set of modes is applied to all 'why' questions of different types of content, while the subcategories vary by content type and sometimes for individual questions.

(ii) An examination of the modes of answering for 'non-why' questions

(a) PREDISPOSING FACTORS GOVERNING THE ANSWERING OF 'WHEN', 'WHERE' AND 'WHO' QUESTIONS

For 'when' and 'where' questions and to some extent 'who', it seems that the situational features which generally bias towards answering in a particular way are two interrelated ones:

1 that of *contiguity* and
2 that of the *associated network of relevance.*

When an event has happened 'recently' it may be more helpful (normal) to refer to the time as 'last week', 'last year', 'two minutes ago' (i.e. mode 2 style), rather than 'November 6th-13th, 1969', or 'twelve minutes past four' (mode 1). Further, in certain situations it may clearly be this sort of information that is more relevant than that in any other mode. An answer which relates the time of an event to, for instance, an individual's age or contemporary occupation assumes these to be relevant to the event. As for time, so also for place; if one requests knowledge of the siting of an object 'near' to oneself one might well expect an indication like 'Just round the corner from here' rather than 'In Stoney Street'. If, however, one were at the other end of the town, it would probably be helpful to have an explicit mention of 'Stoney Street' somewhere in the answer. If the location of one's grandmother were asked for by someone whose concern was with finding out about the geographical proximity of members of kin groups, 'In the same town as me' or 'Two streets away from me' might be more helpful than 'In Eversley' or 'Near a Post Office'.

Some children lived nearer the school (where the questions were posed) than others, and this may have made some difference to mode choice for the question 'Where is your home?' but it could easily be seen by reference to their actual addresses that, given equal distance away, some would say 'In Blank Street' and others would prefer 'Somewhere near here' or 'In a flat'. The placing of the question 'Where does your best friend live?' (Q.4) almost next to 'Where is your home?' (Q.2) required us to modify our scoring, so that if a child answered in such a way that one could infer a mode 1 answer (e.g. by saying 'Next door to me' when the location of the child's own home had been given objective reference), such an answer was included under a mode 1+ category.

A disposition to use a name rather than a role specification for the 'who' questions may be a function of:

(a) how well the person in question is known to the answerer and to the questioner,
(b) what is the customary method of reference,
(c) the answerer's interpretation of the function of the question.

While it may have been partly due to a lack of familiarity that nearly all children gave a simple role specification in answer to Q.12, 'Who

is the man who sees you when you are ill?' all children are assumed
to be reasonably familiar with their teacher. The extent of this
familiarity is also assumed to be more or less equal for all the children.
There was no check on the customs of particular schools or classes
with regard to teacher reference. The third condition (c) is one which
is true not just for this question, but for all the others too.

(b) AN EXAMINATION OF THE VALIDITY OF MODE SEPARA-TIONS FOR ANSWERS TO 'NON-WHY' QUESTIONS (see Tables 10.1, 2 and 3)

The fullest examination of the validity of answering modes for 'non-
why' questions as they apply to individual question types that we
can undertake here is for 'when' questions. This is because they
alone offer alternative possibilities, viz. mode X versus mode other
than X. Thus for 'when' questions we have negative as well as
positive information about the choice of a mode. However, we can
only use this negative information for the objective mode 1, because
this is the only mode which is shared for more than one 'when'
question (Q.1 and Q.18). For Q.18 it is the use of the mode with
more precise content that is separated off rather than the whole of
mode 1, although the mode other than one category is what it claims
to be: it does not contain instances of a vague use of mode 1.

An evaluation of the validity of mode separations for 'where'
questions can use only positive information about the use of mode 1
or 1+. The mode 1+ category was introduced to compensate for a
shortcoming in the design of the experimental material (see p. 124),
and may reduce the strength of positive relationships between modes
1 and 1+ since, although objective information is inferable from
such answers as 'Down my road', it is not known which subjects
were aware of this and which not.

For 'where' questions, then, we simply investigate the relationships
between the various uses of mode 1 or 1+. For 'when' questions we
can do this, and also note the relationship between the mode other
than 1 categories for the two relevant questions as well as the
relationship between mode other than 1 for one question and mode
1 for the other. As Table 10.1 reveals, the boys' results give greater
support for the validity of the separation between mode 1 and mode
other than 1 than do the girls'. The relatively small negative relationship between the precise use of mode 1 for Q.18 and mode other than
1 for Q. 18 might suggest that there were a fair number of vague uses
of an objective mode. This might explain the failure of the negative
relationship between the use of mode 1 for Q.1 and that of mode
other than 1 for Q.18 to reach significance. The relationships for the

TABLE 10.1 *The use of mode 1 for 'when' questions*

	Girls				Boys			
	Q.1, mode 1	Q.1, mode other than 1	Q.18, mode 1a	Q.18, mode other than 1	Q.1, mode 1	Q.1, mode other than 1	Q.18, mode 1a	Q.18, mode other than 1
Q.1, mode 1								
Q.1, mode other than 1	++++ −79				++++ −91			
Q.18, mode 1a	+13	−05			+ +32	++ −41		
Q.18, mode other than 1	+16	−15	+++ −36		−24	+03	−18	

In all the tables of this chapter significance levels are marked in the following way:

$p < 0.10$ + (for girls, $r \geqslant 23$, for boys, $r \geqslant 31$, for total sample, $r \geqslant 18$)
$p < 0.05$ ++ (for girls, $r \geqslant 27$, for boys, $r \geqslant 36$, for total sample, $r \geqslant 21$)
$p < 0.01$ +++ (for girls, $r \geqslant 36$, for boys, $r \geqslant 47$, for total sample, $r \geqslant 28$)
$p < 0.01$ ++++ (for girls, $r \geqslant 44$, for boys, $r \geqslant 58$, for total sample, $r \geqslant 35$)

girls alone do not support the validity of the separation. None of the correlations except the 'forced-choice' ones is significant. In all, however, we have more evidence in support of the separation than against it at this stage. The total sample gives a positive relationship between the use of mode 1 for Q.1 and the precise use of mode 1 for Q.18 ($r = +0.20$, $p < 0.10$).

The only significant relationship between the uses of mode 1 or 1+ for 'where' questions is that for the girls between mode 1 and 1+ for Q.2 and Q.4. Other relationships for both are usually in the positive direction, but not significant. This is not really surprising, in view of the ambiguity of the mode 1+ response. Further, we can examine whether the label 'objective' means something similar for both 'when' and 'where' questions. There is not very strong evidence that this is true, but the two correlations which are statistically significant are supportive of the thesis that there is some common feature.

TABLE 10.2 *The use of mode 1 for 'where' questions*

	Girls			Boys		
	Q.2, mode 1	*Q.4, mode 1+*	*Q.6, mode 1+*	*Q.2, mode 1*	*Q.4, mode 1+*	*Q.6, mode 1+*
Q.2, mode 1						
Q.4, mode 1+	++ +29			+16		
Q.6, mode 1+	−01	+15		+15	+03	

TABLE 10.3 *The use of mode 1 for 'where' and 'when' questions*

	Girls			Boys		
	Q.2, mode 1	*Q.4, mode 1+*	*Q.6, mode 1+*	*Q.2, mode 1*	*Q.4, mode 1+*	*Q.6, mode 1+*
Q.1, mode 1	−06	+10	+08	00	−22	+22
Q.1, mode other than 1	−01	00	−14	−02	+19	−18
Q.18, mode 1a	+ +23	+13	00	+16	+15	+30
Q.18, mode other than 1	−09	+07	+02	++ −42	−15	−18

(c) HIGHER ORDER GROUPINGS OF MODES FOR ANSWERS TO 'NON-WHY' QUESTIONS (see Table 10.4)

Are there any overriding principles whereby we can group different modes together as representing some common viewpoint? The modes we have not yet discussed are mode 3 relative to own age and mode other than 3 for answering Q.11, the unique-person specification in answer to Q.9 and the functional definition mode for Q.10.

For boys, the use of mode 3 for Q.11 relates positively, though not always significantly so, to the use of mode 1 for other 'when' and for 'where' questions, while the mode other than 3 category relates negatively to these, again not always significantly. Girls produce very

TABLE 10.4 *Mode 3 for Q.11 related to mode 1 for other 'when' and 'where' questions*

	Boys						
	Q.1, mode 1	*Q.1, mode other than 1*	*Q.18, mode 1a*	*Q.18, mode other than 1*	*Q.2, mode 1*	*Q.4, mode 1+*	*Q.6, mode 1+*
Q.11, mode 3	+24	−18	+15	−19	+19	++ +41	+21
Q.11, mode other than 3	+ −31	+26	−14	+04	−24	++ −36	−29

small correlations which do not always show, even in a smaller way, the same positive-negative distribution that the boys do. In the light of our earlier discussion (p. 200) about predisposing factors and answering, we might group the use of mode 3 for Q.11 together with that of mode 1 for the other 'when' and for the 'where' questions as representing the more acceptable ways of answering, given the situation in which the questions were asked. A mode 3 answer for Q.11 might also constitute a better way to answer if accurate information is to be given, since children might find it hard to give the year in which they first started school, and we suspect that many who tried to estimate the time from the present gave inaccurate answers.

Mode 3 for Q.11 is the only mode which relates to the unique person specification for Q.9. This is true only for girls and is a minimal relationship ($r = +0.23$, $p < 0.10$). Mode other than 3 relates in the opposite direction ($r = −23$, $p < 0.10$). Both modes have person reference in common, but we cannot say more. A functional definition of school, when related to other modes, suggests no bases for higher groupings.

(iii) An examination of modes of answering 'why' questions

(a) INTRODUCTION (see Table 10.5)

Table 10.5 shows which modes, subcategories and other scoring categories for which responses to which 'why' questions were entered as variables into the matrix.

Generally, as with 'non-why' modes, the scoring categories have shown themselves to be useful in demonstrating social differences in answering behaviour. All the same, it may be that, by using the correlational data that we have, we shall be able to detect indications that, at least for these particular subjects answering these particular questions, certain other separations according to mode might have been more appropriate than some of those which were made. For instance, it may be that categorization functions very similarly to cause in answers to physical questions or that a causal answer to a physical question is not the 'same sort of thing' as a causal answer to one of our social questions. It may be that one of the subcategories within a mode is so different from the others that little common ground can be seen to justify continuing to retain it together with the others within the same mode. Such findings as these will prompt us to re-examine what exactly is involved in answering in a given mode for a given type of question.

Beginning via relationships of subcategories, we shall proceed to seek out those correlations which support the present separations and those which suggest that present divisions between modes are not adequate. The subcategories were not designed for the purpose of demonstrating mode consistency, but they may show up anti-pathetical elements within a mode. Other non-homogeneous elements within a mode may go undetected if no surprising relationships cause us to consider that they might exist.

In our examination of mode and subcategory relationships we shall not restrict our interest simply to relationships with other modes and subcategories. We shall also make use of the scoring category 'irrelevance' as it is applied to physical questions and of the two refusal responses N.A. and D.K. We may be able to infer something about the content or meaning of modes and subcategories from the way in which they relate to these non-mode scoring categories.

(b) AN EXAMINATION OF MODE VALIDITY THROUGH THE RELATIONSHIPS OF SUBCATEGORIES

What we are looking for in this examination of subcategory relationships is any indication of such disunity within a mode that some

c

TABLE 10.5 *Modes and subcategories for answers to 'why' questions of different content types*

	Restatement	Regularity	Authority	Emotions	Categorization	Cause	Purpose	Irrelevance	No answer	'Don't know'
Physical content		Alone			All	All	All	All irrelevance		
Relevant questions		Qualified			categorization	cause	purpose	All		
Relevant responses		No. 23 only			All	All	All	All		
Moral content		First only	Specified	Positive	All	All	All			
			Unspecified	Negative	Simple		All positive, negative actor-oriented punishment, negative actor-oriented, other-ill effect, action-oriented, other-oriented, all actor-oriented, negative general.			
					Object					
					Action					
					Person					
Relevant questions		All	All	All	All	None	All			
					Categorization		Purpose			
					All		All			

Distal

	restatement	regularity	authority	categorization	cause	purpose	no answer	'Don't know'
Relevant questions				All	No. 13 only	All Purpose All	All	All
Relevant responses				All	All	All	All	All
Physical + moral + social content	All	All	All	All	All	All		
Relevant questions	All	All	All	All	All physical + social	All	All	All
Relevant responses	All	All	All	All	All	All	All	All

subcategory could justifiably be said to resemble some other mode rather than the one under which it is presently included. This implies not simply a negative indication which separates it off from the rest of its present mode, but also some positive indication that it belongs elsewhere.

Of course, it may be that we shall find that the only way of coping with some divergent subcategory is to invent a new mode to which it can then belong as part or whole. But what are those indications that a mode contains elements which would be more appropriately placed elsewhere? What we *cannot* necessarily expect as an indicator of homogeneity is a positive correlation between one subcategory and others of the same mode. If the subcategories are to represent some separate orientation within a mode, we must not be surprised if a person who adopts a given orientation does so to the exclusion of a different orientation for any given question. This may extend over questions also, so that we might even expect a negative correlation between subcategories. However, the possibility of giving three responses per question and the frequency of multi-category responding for answers to 'why' questions take some of the exclusive element out of this.

The way in which we shall attempt to discover faulty inclusions within a mode, using our correlation data, is to see if the different subcategories of a mode relate in a similar way:

(A) to different modes and their subcategories both (1) within the same content type and (2) across content type,
(B) to the same mode but across content type.

Diagrammatically, our investigation of the subcategory relationships of a mode can be represented as Fig. 10.1 opposite.

The unfilled box is that which relates the subcategories of a given mode to the same mode within the same content type. This may look like relating the same variable to itself and getting the inevitable $+1\cdot0$ correlation. In fact, it could involve relating subcategories to other subcategories within the same mode and relating separate subcategories to summed scores. For the reasons given above, we are not particularly interested in the relationships between subcategories of a given mode at this point. We may wish to refer to the relationship of a given subcategory to the summed score for a mode as an estimate of the relative frequency of use, for example, but this will be in the context of relating that subcategory to some other mode or to the same mode, but within different content type.

An approach to mode validation via subcategories is obviously essential where we have only subcategories and no summed score for the occurrence of the mode within content type. This is the case

FIG. 10.1 *The pattern for the investigation of the similarity of relationships amongst the subcategories of a mode*

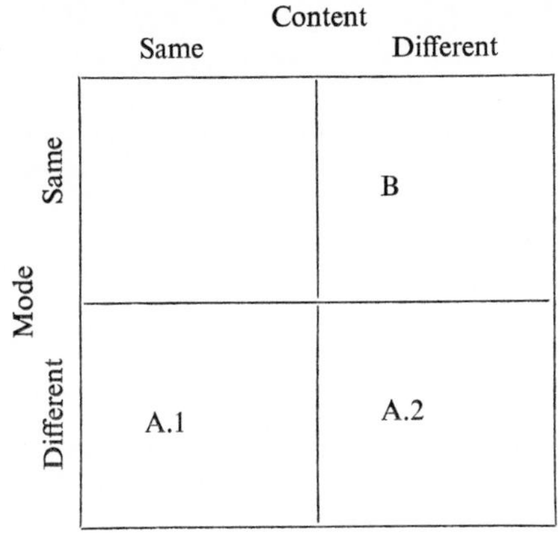

Content

	Same	Different
Same (Mode)		B
Different (Mode)	A.1	A.2

for the authority mode for moral questions, where there are two subcategories 'specified' and 'unspecified'; but no summed score for moral questions, although there is a summed score for the use of this mode across all content types. Likewise, the subcategories 'alone' and 'qualified' for the regularity mode used in the first response to Q.23 and the subcategories 'distal' and 'proximal' used for Q.13 are the only representatives of their modes within their content types (physical and social respectively). An appeal to emotions, which may be either positive or negative for moral questions, has no summed score even for the total content.

It should be noted that not all the subcategories are discrete. The 'simple' subcategory for the moral categorization mode contains a proportion of these response items also included under the action-oriented subcategory and a proportion of those included under the person subcategory. Person and action do not overlap, however. Within moral consequence also there are overlaps. The negative general subcategory contains most of the action-oriented responses (i.e. all those which are negative) as well as items from all the other subcategories except the positive one. The actor-oriented punishment and actor-oriented other ill-effect subcategories are both included under the total actor-oriented subcategory, while the positive subcategory contains items from the action-oriented, actor-oriented and other-oriented subcategories. The subcategories under regularity, authority, emotions and cause do not overlap, however, although the use of certain types of distal cause sometimes makes the use of a proximal cause very likely to occur.

(a) A.1. The relationships between the different subcategories of a mode and different modes and their subcategories within content type.

The comparisons which can be made are as follows:

Physical content

The subcategories of regularity — with *physical* categorization, cause, consequence and (although not a mode) irrelevance

Moral content

The subcategories of authority — with *moral* emotions, categorization, consequence

The subcategories of emotions — with *moral* authority, categorization, consequence

The subcategories of categorization — with *moral* authority, emotions, consequence

The subcategories of consequence — with *moral* authority, emotions, categorization

Social content

The subcategories of cause — with *social* consequence

Discussion of the relationships will follow the order of content and subcategories, represented on the left-hand side of the above list.

A.1. Physical content—regularity (see Table 10.6)

There are no significant differences between the correlations of the two subcategories of regularity alone and qualified when they are related to other modes for physical content questions.

While for boys it is qualified regularity which achieves an almost significant positive correlation with irrelevance ($r = +0.30$, not sig.) rather than regularity alone ($r = +0.10$), for girls it is regularity alone which has a similar slight positive correlation ($r = +0.24$, $p < 0.10$) and not regularity qualified ($r = -0.03$). For neither sex are the two subcategories significantly differently related to irrelevance. The difference between boys and girls may be a reflection of a differential frequency of use. This is suggested by the relationships of the two with total content regularity.

In the tables of this chapter, correlations which are significantly different, ($p < 0.05$), from others in the same column or row may be marked '*' or '†'. Where more than one other correlation is significantly different from a third, the relative size of the numbers will indicate which is different from which. Where there is only one set of significant differences within one column or row, '*' will be used for each relevant correlation. Where there are two sets both '*' and '†' will be used, one for each set.

TABLE 10.6 *The subcategories of regularity related to total content regularity*

	Girls			Boys		
	Q.23, R.1 regularity	*Alone*	*Qualified*	*Q.23, R.1 regularity*	*Alone*	*Qualified*
Total regularity		++++ +63*	+16*		+18	++ +54

Moreover, when total content regularity is related to irrelevance, the significance levels which obtained for the different subcategories by the two sexes are certainly not reduced (boys, $r = +0.36, p < 0.05$; girls, $r = +0.27, p < 0.05$).

So far, then, we have more evidence for similarity than dissimilarity between the two subcategories of regularity if we look at their relationships for the total sample.

A1. Moral content—authority

There are no significant differences in the relationships of the two authority subcategories specified and unspecified with other modes and subcategories of moral content. Where there is a significant correlation between one of the authority subcategories and another scoring category, the other subcategory relates in the same direction, though not significantly. This is true at least within each sex group. It may be that one subcategory tends to emphasize some aspect more than the other, but such speculation must await further evidence.

A1. Moral content—emotions (see Table 10.7)

The positive and negative subcategories of an appeal to emotions might not be expected to differ much from one another, especially to the extent of resembling some other mode. However, something more may be involved than a simple response to the polarity of the question.

For girls the positive and negative subcategories are not significantly dissimilar in their relationships with other modes and subcategories within moral content. Moreover, relationships with the subcategories of consequence are all positive (though not all significantly so) for both subcategories. Thus, not surprisingly they both relate positively with the summed consequence mode (positive, $r = +0.28$, $p < 0.05$; negative, $r = +0.38$, $p < 0.01$).

For boys the two subcategories are differently related to the simple and action subcategories of categorization. Positive emotions have significant negative relationships with both simple ($r = -0.56$, $p < 0.01$) and action ($r = -0.48$, $p < 0.01$) categorization which are not shared by negative emotions (simple, $r = +0.15$; action, $r = +0.10$; z diffs., $p < 0.05$).

It may be remembered that the action and simple subcategories of categorization are not discrete, and both refer to such utterances as 'Because it is naughty', which account for quite a large proportion of each subcategory. Why should subjects who give such reasons be so unlikely to make an appeal to positive emotions and yet not unlikely to make an appeal to negative emotions? What is involved in an appeal to positive emotions which is not in an appeal to negative emotions? It is difficult to say at present. A further examination of subcategory relationships may throw light upon this.

TABLE 10.7 *The subcategories of emotions related to consequence*

	Boys							
	M. consequence: Positive	Actor-oriented, punishment	Actor-oriented, other ill-effect	All actor-oriented,	Action-oriented	Other-oriented	Negative general	All M. consequence
M. emotions								
Positive	−20	+12	+06	+17	* −22	++* +46	* −05	+28
Negative	+30	−11	+01	+11	++++* +59	* −09	++* +46	+30

The relationships between the two subcategories of emotions and the moral consequence mode and its subcategories for boys is best represented as a table. The difference in relationship with positive consequence between positive and negative emotions almost reaches the 5 per cent level of significance. It is the opposite way round from what one might imagine. It seems to suggest that sequences involving a combination of positive emotions and the consequence mode, e.g. 'They want them to be happy' are not common. Other significant differences are with the action-oriented subcategory with which negative emotions achieves a high positive correlation ($p < 0.001$) which is not shared by positive emotions (z diff., $p < 0.05$). For the negative general subcategory a similar significant difference exists, while for the other-oriented subcategory it is positive emotions which achieves a significantly different positive relationship.

It is unfortunate that we chose simply to break the emotions mode on polarity, since that is a most difficult dimension to make sense of without the aid of further information. If, for instance, we knew whether the emotions referred to were those of the actor or of some other, then these other relationships might be more explicable. If we had more information about the use of the mode as to whether it were being used indirectly or directly (see Appendix B, p. 330), this would be particularly useful for understanding relationships with the consequence mode, which was the mode most frequently used with an indirect use of emotions. Furthermore, lacking any variable representing summed emotions, we have no idea of the relative proportions of each subcategory, nor how much each is dependent upon the polarity of the question. All we can do for the moment is to bear in mind these differences in the way the two subcategories relate to other moral content modes and subcategories, and note any further evidence that clarifies what it is that separates the two in this way.

A1. Moral content—categorization (see Tables 10.8 and 9)

The subcategory of categorization which is most conspicuous for the way in which it relates differently from the rest of the mode to the other modes and subcategories of moral content is object categorization.

For girls the only significant difference is between the subcategories object ($r = +0.28$, $p < 0.05$) and persons ($r = -0.23$, $p < 0.10$) in their relations with negative emotions (z diff., $p < 0.05$). Neither subcategory differs significantly from the simple and action subcategories in this relationship (simple, $r = +0.03$; action, $r = +0.08$).

For boys the negative correlation between the simple and action subcategories and positive emotions has already been mentioned. In this these two subcategories differ from the person and object subcategories. The difference between object categorization and other subcategories emerges when the subcategories are related to the consequence mode and its subcategories. It can be seen that among the generally negatived relationships between categorization and consequence subcategories other than positive object categorization move towards more positive relationships.

What is it that might make object categorization differ from other subcategories of categorization in its more positive or less negative association with negative emotions (for girls) and positive emotions

TABLE 10.8 *The subcategories of categorization related to positive emotions*

	Boys			
	M. categorization: Simple	*Object*	*Action*	*Person*
M. emotions: positive	+++* −56	†* +04	+++† −48	* 00

TABLE 10.9 *The subcategories of categorization related to consequence*

	Boys							
	M. consequence: Positive	*Actor-oriented, punishment*	*Actor-oriented, other ill-effect*	*All actor-oriented*	*Action-oriented*	*Other-oriented*	*Negative general*	*All M. consequence*
M. categorization:								
Simple	+27	−17	+ −34	++ −37	+17	* −27	−16	+* −35
Object	−03	−03	+09	−02	+22	++* +42	+* +32	* +18
Action	+20	−19	++ −38	++ −41	+13	* −30	* −20	++* −40
Person	−08	−06	+ −33	−26	−16	* −16	−18	+ −33

and consequence (for boys)? It may be that object categorization lends itself to further explication in terms of wants and consequences. Thus, when a subject suggests that a reason for avoiding stealing is the fact that the object belongs to someone else or is of value to them, he may go on to explain how the owner would suffer disappointment or loss if the object were stolen from him. Such a further explication may be in response to a probe, such as 'Why should you not take another person's property?' On the other hand, it may be that such considerations of wants and consequences are implied rather than explicated by those who make object categorizations; subjects who recognize the rights of others and the duty to respect such rights are showing a similar attitude to that which is concerned about consequences for others when their rights are not respected.

A1. Moral content—consequence (see Table 10.10)

For girls the subcategories of consequence generally have very similar relationships with the other modes and subcategories of moral content.

The two significant divergences both involve the actor-oriented, other ill-effect subcategory. It differs from action-oriented consequence in having a more positive relationship with unspecified authority (actor-oriented other ill-effect, $r = + 0.23$, $p < 0.10$; action-oriented, $r = -0.24$, $p < 0.10$; z diff., $p < 0.05$). It is also significantly more positive than other-oriented consequence in its relationship with person categorization (actor-oriented other ill-effect, $r = + 0.23$, $p < 0.10$; other-oriented, $r = -0.20$, not sig.; z diff., $p < 0.05$). There seems to be no obvious explanation for these divergences at this stage of the analysis.

For the boys, positive consequence sometimes differs from other subcategories of consequence when related to other modes and subcategories of moral content. Where this is true, the action-oriented subcategory generally moves in the same direction as positive consequence.

Perhaps those items which are scored under positive consequence tend to be of the more general (action-oriented) sort. Negative emotions could be construed as implying a very general sort of consequence in so far as one might refrain from doing something so as to avoid disappointing one's own or someone else's wishes. The failure to find a parallel relationship with positive emotions forbids us to draw such a conclusion at all firmly, though.

It may be that the more positive associations that simple and action categorization have with the positive and action-oriented subcate-

TABLE 10.10 *The subcategories of consequence related to emotions and simple and action categorization*

	Boys						
	M. consequence: Positive	*Actor-oriented, punishment*	*Actor-oriented, other ill-effects*	*All actor-oriented*	*Action-oriented*	*Other-oriented*	*Negative general*
M. emotions							
Positive	* −20	+12	+06	+17	* −22	++* +46	−05
Negative	+30	+11	+01	+11	++++* +59	* −09	++* +46
M. categorization:							
Simple	* +27	−17	+* −34	++* −37	+17	* −27	−16
Action	* +20	−19	++* −38	++* −41	+13	−30	−20

gories is due to the inclusion of responses which see obeying parents as leading to 'doing the right things etc.' under the positive action-oriented subcategory (see Appendix B p. 334). Such responses have a similar concern to that of the simple and action subcategories of categorization with actions being good and right. Another explanation may lie in the relatively non-specific impersonal aspect which those subcategories may all share.

Finally in this section A.1, we must examine the subcategory relationships of social cause with the only other scoring category which exists for social content alone, the mode consequence.

A1. Social content—cause

The correlations for the distal and proximal subcategories of social cause with social consequence are positive, none of them significantly so, for both sexes. There is certainly no significant difference between them in this relationship.

A summary of findings for within content subcategory relationships as they are relevant to the validity of mode separations might be helpful to have at this point.

A1. Summary

Physical content

The two subcategories of the regularity mode give more evidence of similarity than dissimilarity at this stage.

Moral content

The two subcategories of the authority mode suggest different emphases rather than different points of view.

Certain differential relationships of the two subcategories, positive and negative emotions, as they are used by the boys, to subcategories of the categorization and consequence modes are rather mystifying. They may be associated with some difference in content between Q.29, the only moral question posed in the positive polarity (and therefore more likely to evoke positive polarity responses) and the other three moral questions. Further breaks according to whose emotions are being referred to and whether they are directly or indirectly applied (see Appendix B, p. 330) might shed further light on these differences.

Object categorization gives evidence of being associated more positively or less negatively with emotions and consequence modes than are other subcategories of categorization. This may be due to the further explication which tends to follow an appeal to considerations of property or value or it may be that such a categorization is not so opposed to a concern with wants and consequences as are other forms of categorization.

Why the actor-oriented other ill-effect subcategory of consequence is more closely associated with unspecified authority and person categorization than its fellows is not understood at this stage.

It may be that for the boys of the sample the positive and action subcategories of consequence possess elements of greater generality and impersonality which differentiate them from other consequence subcategories and make them more like negative emotions and simple and action categorization than are the other subcategories.

Social content

The two subcategories of cause have similar relationships with social consequence.

Our failure to find any single convincing explanations prevents us from making even tentative alterations of mode boundaries before seeking further evidence from the comparison of subcategory relationships with modes and subcategories of different content type.

(b) *A2. The relationships between the different subcategories of a mode and different modes and their subcategories across content type*

The comparisons which can be made are as follows:

Physical content

The subcategories of regularity — with *Moral* authority, emotions, categorization, consequence
social cause, consequence
total restatement, authority, categorization, cause, consequence, N.A., D.K.

Moral content

The subcategories of authority — with *physical* regularity, categorization, cause, consequence, irrelevance
social cause, consequence
total restatement, regularity, categorization, cause, consequence, N.A., D.K.

The subcategories of emotions — with *physical* regularity, categorization, cause, consequence, irrelevance
social cause, consequence
total restatement, regularity, authority, categorization, cause, consequence, N.A., D.K.

The subcategories of categorization — with *physical* regularity, cause, consequence, irrelevance
social cause, consequence
total restatement, regularity, authority, cause, consequence, N.A., D.K.

The subcategories of consequence — with *physical* regularity, categorization, cause, irrelevance
social cause
total restatement, regularity authority, categorization, cause, N.A., D.K.

Social content

The subcategories of social cause — with *physical* regularity, categorization, consequence, irrelevance
moral authority, emotions, categorization, consequence
total restatement, regularity, authority, categorization, consequence, N.A., D.K.

There are certain difficulties involved in cross-content comparisons. A given scoring category may not have quite the same meaning for different content types, though we shall be investigating this problem as it applies to a limited number of modes (see p. 236). Again, a given mode may have more limited applicability within one content type than within the others. Hence, although the causal mode is not relevant to moral questions, we still try to make sense of the way that, for instance, the positive and negative general subcategories of moral consequence are related differently from one another to distal cause for social content. Furthermore, responses to questions of one content type may spread over a greater range of scoring categories than those to questions of a different content type.

Presumed advantages of cross-content comparisons in general include that of a relative independence of variables because within-content comparisons tend to have reduced positive correlations since a subject who has answered one way has 'used up time' that could have been spent answering in another way. It may be that such an effect does hold here, but slightly, since, as we have already mentioned (p. 186), it is reduced by the number of questions and of responses per question. As far as our present analysis is concerned, we require the additional evidence especially since we were unable to include all modes for all content types. If, for instance, we did not compare the subcategories of regularity in relation to moral and total authority we could not compare them in relation to any authority.

Among the 'different' content types we include total content. This, of course, may include the same content as that of the mode under examination, so that the content is only partly different in fact.

The order of discussion will again follow that exhibited on the left-hand side of the above list.

A2. Physical content—regularity (see Tables 10.11 and 12)

For both girls and boys, regularity alone shows a pattern of predominantly negative correlations with other scoring categories for each content type, although some of these are slight. Exceptions include relationships with authority, restatement and N.A.

Significant differences between the two subcategories are found in their relationships with the consequence mode for both moral and total content.

It might be worth mentioning the positive relationship between regularity alone and restatement for boys ($r = +0.33$, $p < 0.05$), but this is not significantly different from that of regularity qualified ($r = -0.04$).

There are significant differences for both sexes when the two subcategories are related to the 'failure to respond' scoring categories, D.K. and N.A. For both sexes regularity alone is related positively to N.A. For girls, regularity qualified is related to positively with D.K.

The above pattern of relationships suggests that regularity alone might be the sort of response given by subjects who are reluctant to

TABLE 10.11 *The subcategories of regularity related to consequence*

	Girls		Boys	
	Q. 23, R.1, regularity: Alone	*Qualified*	*Q. 23, R.1, regularity: Alone*	*Qualified*
M. consequence:				
Actor-oriented Punishment	+ −24	−15	−03	+++ +47
Other-oriented	−19	+05	−20	+16
All M. consequence	++ −32	−06	* −22	* +30
S. consequence	+ −24	−12	++ −42	+06
T. consequence	++ −33	−02	+* −31	* +28

	Total sample	
	Q.23, R.1, regularity: Alone	*Qualified*
M. consequence:		
Actor-oriented, punishment	* −14	+* +20
Other-oriented	++* −21	* +16
All M. consequence	++* −27	* +15
S. consequence	+++ −28	−04
T. consequence	+++* −30	* +16

TABLE 10.12 *The subcategories of regularity related to refusal responses*

	Girls		Boys	
	Q. 23, R.1, regularity: Alone	*Qualified*	*Q. 23, R.1, regularity: Alone*	*Qualified*
T. refusals: N.A.	+* +25	* −21	+++* +47	* −15
D.K.	* −03	+++* +37	−18	+05

say anything at all and are perhaps uncertain about what they do and do not know. Our problem is to decide whether it is the brevity of such an answer that is relevant to such an association or whether it is the assumed satisfactoriness of an answer which simply appeals to the regularity of an event, as though such an appeal were an explanation rather than mentioning it as part of a fuller attempt at explanation. Whatever the reason behind it, there is undeniable evidence of a cleavage here. Further examination of the various other subcategories may enable us to set this into a fuller picture.

A2. Moral content—authority

For the girls, specified and unspecified authority differ significantly in their relationships with social consequence (specified, $r = +0.44$, $p < 0.001$; unspecified, $r = -0.02$; z diff., $p < 0.05$). The difference in their relationships with physical consequence misses the 5 per cent level of significance (specified, $r = +0.17$; unspecified, $r = -0.20$).

For boys it is physical cause which separates specified ($r = +0.37$, $p < 0.05$) from unspecified ($r = -0.17$, not sig.) authority (z diff., $p < 0.05$). Positive relationships between *each* subcategory and both physical and total cause for girls and the positive relationship between unspecified authority and physical consequence ($r = +0.33, p < 0.10$) for boys forbids any hasty generalizations about specified authority belonging within a cause-consequence cluster.

As for regularity alone, there is a positive relationship between

D

unspecified authority and restatement ($r = +0\cdot30$, $p < 0\cdot05$), although this is not significantly different from that of specified authority ($r = -0\cdot01$). This time it is the girls who show the relationship.

At the moment we can still maintain only that there is a difference in emphasis, specified authority having more in common with causal and consequence modes.

A2. Moral content—emotions (see Tables 10.13 and 14)

The positive and negative subcategories of emotion differ in relation to social consequence. For some reason, such responses as 'So that he doesn't grow a beard' in response to Q.21 tend to be given or are

TABLE 10.13   *The subcategories of emotions related to consequence*

	Girls	Boys	Total sample
	S. consequence	S. consequence	S. consequence
M. emotions:			
Positive		*	*
	+09	−08	+01
Negative	++	++*	++++*
	+35	+46	+39

given in greater number by subjects who say 'Because X wants Y'. We are again handicapped by ignorance about whose emotions are being referred to and whether they are attached to a consequence or not. Certainly the link between negative emotions and consequence as far as answers to those of our questions with human content is concerned is further supported here.

The other differential relationship is with total content categorization.

For boys this is a result of the negative relationship between physical categorization and positive emotions ($r = -0\cdot34$, $p < 0\cdot10$)

TABLE 10.14 *The subcategories of emotions related to categorization*

	Girls	Boys	Total sample
	T. categorization	*T. categorization*	*T. categorization*
M. emotions:			
Positive	−15	++* −40	* −17
Negative	+16	* +12	* +14

as well as that between positive emotions and the simple ($r = -0.56$, $p < 0.01$) and action ($r = -0.48$, $p < 0.01$) subcategories of moral categorization which we noted in the previous section.

A2. Moral content—categorization (see Tables 10.15, 16 and 17)

The subcategory differences for the girls are between the person and action subcategories of categorization and physical and social consequence and N.A. Only those associated with social consequence reach significance. The differential relationship with consequence may be explicable purely in terms of that with N.A. Social consequence correlates negatively with N.A. ($r = -0.36$, $p < 0.05$), and so does physical consequence ($r = -0.35$, $p < 0.05$). Subjects who supply person categorization are subjects who less frequently answer questions than are those who give action categorizations (the most commonly used subcategory). Why should this be so? It may be that the particular-person categorization involved are those which refer to actual rather than contingent attributes, e.g. 'Because they *are small*' rather than 'Because you'll *be naughty*'. Where the contingent attributes are sufficiently general, e.g. 'naughty', 'wrong', 'good', they are also included under the simple subcategory. Quite probably, reference to fixed actual attributes is a rule which has been learned, often without understanding of the reasons behind it.

TABLE 10.15 *The subcategories of categorization related to consequence and N.A.*

	Girls			
	M. categorization: Simple	*Object*	*Action*	*Person*
P. consequence	+12	+05	+17	−20
S. consequence	++ +28	+08	+++* +37	* −08
T. N. A.	−13	00	++ −30	+07

TABLE 10.16 *The subcategories of categorization related to cause and consequence*

	Boys					
	P. cause	*S. cause: Proximal*	*Distal*	*T. cause (P+S)*	*S. consequence*	*T. consequence*
M. categorization:						
Simple	−01	* −06	−11	* +01	+16	−15
Object	+ +33	+++* +54	+29	+++* +54	+20	* +22
Action	−06	* −10	−07	* −02	+10	−20
Person	−11	* −01	+04	* −04	−29	+* −33

The relatively small number of divergent relationships encourages us to think of the categorization made as more or less homogeneous as it is used by girls.

The boys continue to demonstrate a difference between object categorization and the other subcategories of categorization, this time in its greater tendency to relate positively with cause and consequence modes.

In some ways it might be thought that object categorization would resemble restatement rather than occur with the generally more acceptable explanations, such as cause and consequence. It does, after all, frequently consist of a mention of the fact of property, which is implied anyhow by the word 'steal'. A notion of stealing is dependent upon one of property. But then other categorization responses, such as 'Because it's being naughty', could also be considered synonymous with 'You should not do it', and thus be a type of restatement. Relations of the subcategories of categorization to restatement are all positive, but non-significant.

TABLE 10.17 *The subcategories of categorization related to restatement*

| | Boys | | | |
	M. categorization: Simple	Object	Action	Person
T. restatement	+13	+28	+18	+23

It seems clear that, in the way that the modes and subcategories are used for the boys, an appeal to property rights or value is associated with a disposition not so opposed as other categorizations to seeking explanations in the network of empirical relationships prior to or subsequent to the event in question. It is the subcategory of categorization which is most likely to introduce two elements which are not explicitly mentioned in the question—namely, the object to be stolen and the person who owns it. These two are related together via the categorization of the object as the person's property or as valuable to them (although in this case 'to them' may only be implied). Thus, although such a response has a kinship with restatement, it may, nevertheless, for the child who gives it, involve a more complicated investigation of relationships than other forms of categorization. How far this difference may apply beyond the present subjects it is difficult to say. It is not even true for the girls of the sample.

A2. Moral content—consequence (see Tables 10.18 and 19)

For girls the actor-oriented subcategories relate rather differently from the rest of the consequence mode with uses of the modes categorization, restatement and authority. This pattern involves

TABLE 10.18 *The subcategories of consequence related to restatement, authority and categorization*

	Girls						
	M. consequence: Positive	*Actor-oriented, punishment*	*Actor-oriented, other ill-effect*	*All actor-oriented*	*Action-oriented*	*Other-oriented*	*Negative general*
P. categorization	* −20	+17	+18	* +20	+10	−05	+13
T. restatement	−05	++ +28	+20	++* +30	−08	* −19	−05
T. authority	+01	+ +24	+++* +40	++++* +47	* −08	+10	+01

relatively little divergencies and is particularly interesting, since it may well be explicable in terms of the procedures used to control certain of the children. It is characteristic of such procedures that a child's actions are easily categorized by the relevant authority figure, who further emphasizes the power of her position with appeals like 'Because I say so' and by threatening that harm will come to the child if the injunction is disobeyed. There is not enough evidence to justify the separation of the actor-oriented subcategory from the rest of the consequence mode. The differential relations we do find illustrate the value of such a subcategorization.

For boys it is the positive subcategory which relates differently from other subcategories of consequence. The positive subcategory of consequence certainly seems to lean in an opposite and negative direction from certain of the other subcategories when related to regularity and cause. It is difficult to see why this should be except by assuming, as we suggested earlier (p. 217), that positive consequences tend, for boys at least, to be more of the general, impersonal categorical sort, although the action-oriented subcategory does not relate in a similar way to cause. For the girls, as Table 10.18 shows,

TABLE 10.19 *The subcategories of consequence related to regularity and cause*

	Boys						
	M. consequence: Positive	Actor-oriented, punishment	Actor-oriented, other ill-effects	All actor-oriented	Action-oriented	Other-oriented	Negative general
Q23 R1 regularity: qualified	* −26	+++* +47	† −24	++†* +42	−11	+16	−03
S. cause: distal	* −20	−01	+22	+03	+30	+* +34	++* +45
T. regularity	+* −32	+* +32	* +17	++* +42	−12	+13	+04
T. cause	−01	+05	+01	+06	+20	+++ +52	+ +32

there is not much evidence of a positive association between positive consequence and physical categorization. Furthermore, a positive relationship between distal cause and positive consequence ($r = +0.32$, $p < 0.05$) is another indication that either the subcategory positive consequence or those to which it is related do not function similarly for the boys and the girls.

A2. Social content—cause (see Tables 10.20, 21 and 22)

For girls the two subcategories differ significantly in relation to other-oriented moral consequence (proximal, $r = -0.09$; distal,

$r = +0.35 \, p < 0.05$; z diff., $p < 0.05$) and total moral consequence (proximal, $r = 0 -0.02$; distal, $r = +0.39$, $p < 0.01$; z diff., $p < 0.05$). Thus it seems that distal cause, as well as carrying more of an authority element than proximal cause, also has an element in common with the moral consequence mode.

For boys both subcategories have generally positive relationships with the subcategories of moral consequence. These only reach significance for distal cause.

TABLE 10.20 *The subcategories of cause related to consequence*

| | Boys | | | | | | | |
	M. consequence: Positive	Actor-oriented, punishment	Actor-oriented, other ill-effects	All actor-oriented	Action-oriented	Other-oriented	Negative general	All M. consequence
S. cause:								
Proximal	+04	+07	−04	+06	+20	+21	+27	+17
Distal	* −20	−01	+22	+03	+30	+* +34	++* +45	+30

Although, for boys, the difference in relationship which proximal and distal cause have with physical irrelevance does not reach significance (proximal, $r = +0.40$, $p < 0.05$; distal, $r = 0.00$; z diff., not sig.), if we compare the relationship of proximal cause *for boys* with irrelevance to the relationship of distal cause *for girls* with irrelevance ($r = -0.06$) we do get a significant difference (z diff., $p < 0.05$).

The differential relationship between the two subcategories and the authority mode is interesting. If we compare the relationship to specified authority of proximal cause for boys with that of distal cause for girls we get a difference which is almost significant. Why should subjects who make authority responses give distal causes for illness? Perhaps many of the particular distal causes, especially those which are not connected to specific illnesses, are accepted on authority, e.g. 'If you get wet or cold you might be ill'.

There is some evidence of a closer affinity of proximal causes to restatements. The difference is not significant for either sex, but if we again make a cross-sex comparison and compare distal cause for boys with proximal cause for girls we do get a significant relationship (z diff., $p < 0.05$).

Again the number of similar relationships makes us hesitate to reassess what should be called a social cause yet there is a marked difference in emphasis.

TABLE 10.21   *The subcategories of cause related to authority*

	Girls		Boys	
	S. cause: Proximal	*Distal*	*S. cause: Proximal*	*Distal*
M. authority:				
Specified	+03	+ +23	−22	+21
Unspecified	+18	++ +27	+* −31	* +28
T. authority	+17	+++ +36	++* −42	* +14

	Total sample	
	S. cause: Proximal	*Distal*
M. authority:		
Specified	−07	+ +20
Unspecified	* −06	+++* +30
T. authority	* −09	+++* +28

TABLE 10.22   *The subcategories of cause related to restatement*

	Girls		Boys	
	S. cause: Proximal	*Distal*	*S. cause: Proximal*	*Distal*
T. restatement	++ +35	+01	00	−17

This completes the examination of the relationships of mode subcategories with different modes of different content type. Findings will be summarized before we proceed to the final section relevant to the evaluation of mode separations on the basis of subcategory relationships.

A2. Summary

Physical content

Regularity alone differs from regularity qualified in being positively associated with the N.A. type of refusal response rather than the D.K. It also has more negative relationships with scoring categories other than N.A., restatement and authority, and particularly with moral and total consequence. It may well be misleading to group the two subcategories together as representing a single mode, although precise reasons for the divergence are ambiguous.

Moral content

Specified authority seems to have more in common than unspecified authority with cause and consequence modes, though not sufficient to suggest that both do not represent the same basic point of view.

Negative emotion seems to be more positively associated with social consequence and less negatively associated with total categorization than positive emotions. Ignorance of details still prevents us from suggesting alterations.

Girls show some variation in relationships between action and person subcategories of categorization, but these do not justify the removal of either subcategory. Boys continue to show different relationships for object categorization as opposed to other subcategories of categorization. This may be a function of the psychological nature of the task involved, so that for the boys of this sample appeals to property or value may involve similar operations to those involved in supplying cause and consequence responses. Although it might be misleading to label such an appeal a consequence or a cause, yet it would be a mistake not to recognize a radical difference between it and the other sorts of categorization for answers to moral questions.

Girls show some differential relationships between actor-oriented and other subcategories of consequence which do not suggest, however, that changes should be made in the constitution of the mode consequence, but which may be a direct result of different parental (or other) procedures used in controlling and communicating with children. For boys it is positive consequence which again differs from the others, but inexplicably as yet.

Social content

Distal cause has a stronger positive association with authority than does proximal cause. At the same time, it is more closely related to consequence and less likely to be associated with restatement. It seems to be a difference of emphasis rather than one of kind that separates these two subcategories.

So far only two modes have been shown to have subcategories whose correlates suggest a need to modify the coding scheme. In spite of within-content comparisons which point the other way, regularity alone seems to mean something consistently different from regularity qualified, and object categorization seems not to fit in with its fellow subcategories as the boys use these.

The final section using subcategories is a small one, since it is limited to relationships with the same mode albeit across content type.

(c) *B. The relationships between the different subcategories of a mode and the same mode across content type* (The comparisons which can be made are as follows:

Physical content
The subcategories of regularity	with *total* regularity

Moral content
The subcategories of authority	with *total* authority
The subcategories of categorization	with *physical* categorization
	total categorization
The subcategories of consequence	with *physical* consequence
	social consequence
	total consequence

Social content
The subcategories of cause	with *physical* cause
	total cause

B. Physical content—regularity

We have already mentioned (see Table 10.5, p. 206) the differential relationships between the two regularity subcategories as they are related to total regularity, and how they are opposite for the two sex groups.

Whether this means that girls who use regularity qualified in their first response to Q.23 are less likely to use regularity of either sort elsewhere or whether it means that regularity alone represents a significantly greater proportion of regularity responses it is difficult to say. Whatever the case, we can call regularity alone a more 'typical' use of regularity than is regularity qualified when used by the girls.

B. Moral content—authority (see Table 10.23)

The positive relationship between total authority and unspecified moral authority is significantly greater than that between total authority and specified moral authority for both sexes.

TABLE 10.23   *The subcategories of authority related to authority*

	Girls		Boys	
	M. authority: Specified	*Unspecified*	*M. authority: Specified*	*Unspecified*
T. authority	* +12	++++* +78	* +21	++++* +87

Total authority consists of predominantly moral content responses. The most likely explanation for the difference is that a greater proportion of the authority responses were of the unspecified kind.

B. Moral content—categorization (see Table 10.24)

An examination of the relationships of moral categorization subcategories with total moral categorization shows that the action and simple subcategories are the most strongly associated—a reflection of their greater frequency. The differences between the subcategories in relation to physical categorization are not significant. For girls the only significant relationship with physical categorization is for the person subcategory, while those subcategories most typical of moral categorization, simple and action, have a practically zero correlation. For boys, though, they are positively correlated, and so is the person subcategory.

TABLE 10.24　*The subcategories of categorization related to categorization*

	Girls				Boys			
	M. categorization: Simple	*Object*	*Action*	*Person*	*M. categorization: Simple*	*Object*	*Action*	*Person*
M. categorization	++++ +66	+++ +41	++++ +83	+21	++++ +86	++ +36	++++ +90	+30
P. categorization	+01	+21	−02	++ +30	+++ +51	+10	+++ +49	++ +38

Perhaps for the girls it is that subset of person categorizations referring to actual rather than contingent attributes (see p. 223) that is responsible for the relationship with physical categorization, since physical categorization is more likely to be concerned with actual than contingent attributes. Alternatively, it may be that physical categorization is likely to be applied to a participant in the action or event rather than to the action itself, and in this way is like person categorization. Whatever the reason, such a distinction does not seem relevant for the boys.

In this instance object categorization is associated in a similar direction to the other subcategories for the boys, although it lags behind possibly because it has more in common with the use of cause ($r = +0.33$, $p < 0.10$) than of categorization for answers to physical questions.

B. Moral content—consequence

There are no significant differences among moral consequence sub-categories in their relationships with other content consequence within either sex group. Relationships are generally positive, but those between moral consequence subcategories and physical consequence tend rather to be negative for boys. However, that sort of relationship is the subject of a later section.

B. Social content—cause (see Table 10.25)

Relationships between the proximal and distal subcategories and physical cause are positive. Among the girls, distal cause is significantly different from proximal cause in its relationship with total

TABLE 10.25 *The subcategories of cause related to cause*

	Girls		Boys	
	S. cause: Proximal	*Distal*	*S. cause: Proximal*	*Distal*
P. cause	$+09$	$+++$ $+40$	$+28$	$+12$
T. cause	$+*$ $+25$	$++++*$ $+70$	$+++$ $+55$	$++$ $+36$

cause (z diff., $p < 0.05$). Total cause, it may be remembered, consists only of physical and social, not moral content. We may say then that for the girls of our sample distal causes represent more typical causes than do proximal ones. This is not true for the boys.

B. Summary

Physical content

No new evidence of difference between the subcategories of regularity was gleaned through relating them to total-content regularity.

Regularity alone seems the more characteristic use of regularity for the girls of the sample, while the qualified use of regularity seems the more characteristic for the boys.

Moral content

All that can be inferred from relating the subcategories of moral authority with total authority is the relative rarity of the use of specified authority for both sexes.

There are no significant differences in the relationships of categorization subcategories with physical categorization, although for the girls the simple and action subcategories are remarkable for their failure to have any positive association.

The subcategories of consequence are similar to one another in their relationships with other content type instances of consequence.

Social content

Proximal cause seems for girls to be less characteristic as a cause than distal cause.

We are now in a position to draw some conclusions on the basis of our analysis of subcategory relationships.

A1, A2, B. Conclusions Although there are several differing relationships among subcategories, these have for the most part been insufficiently consistent or meaningful to suggest alteration of the scheme of analysis at the more fundamental mode level.

The varying relationships of the positive and negative subcategories of emotions remain inexplicable without further information as to their content.

Although we may separate regularity alone from regularity qualified on the basis of its consistently more negative relationship with other scoring categories, we cannot be sure that this separation is not a function of a tendency to give shorter answers or no answers rather than of some 'point of view' of the answerer.

The way that object categorization can differ from its fellow-subcategories, particularly in relation to cause and consequence modes, prompts us to consider the importance of understanding modes according to what is involved *for the answerer* in answering in a certain way. Thus what might amount to a simple tautology for an adult answerer may for a child constitute a discovery about the world and be arrived at via empirical rather than purely logical operations. The difficulty of such an enterprise is illustrated by the suggestion that the different modes and subcategories do not always even mean the same thing for the boys of the sample as they do for the girls.

Our later grouping into higher-order categories will take into consideration the differences in emphasis which have been manifested by such subcategories as specified versus unspecified authority and proximal versus distal cause.

Certain other suggestions, such as that positive consequence may contain more impersonal, general and categorical elements than other subcategories, we simply bear in mind until further light can be shed, always recognizing that the peculiar content of the relevant questions might be responsible for correlations which are difficult to interpret, while others may be due purely to chance.

Mode validation continues with an examination of relationships of summed modes.

(c) AN EXAMINATION OF MODE VALIDITY THROUGH THE RELATIONSHIPS OF SUMMED MODES

In this section, bearing in mind what we have discovered about the various subcategories and using the same approach, we shall attempt to discover:

1 Whether the same modes of different content type relate together in similar ways such that, for instance, the subjects who make greater use of the categorization mode for answering moral questions also make greater use of the categorization mode for answering physical questions.

2 Whether the different content type uses of the same mode have similar 'external' relationships, such that, for instance, categorization mode for moral content and the categorization mode for physical content relate in a similar way to the causal mode for social content.

1 *Relationships of modes with the same mode of different content type* The only possibilities we have for any sensible comparisons are for the three modes categorization, cause and consequence. The information we gain from such comparisons as that of the two subcategories of Q.23, regularity in relation to total regularity, and two subcategories of moral authority in relation to total authority (which have anyhow already been made) is not informative in this context, since we do not have summed mode scores for more than one content type.

Categorization (see Table 10.26)

For girls the relationship between physical and moral categorization is positive, but non-significant. We have already noted the failure of the simple and action subcategories to correlate positively with physical categorization.

Boys show a fairly strong positive correlation between the two content type uses.

TABLE 10.26 *Categorization related to categorization*

	Girls			Boys		
	P. categorization	*M. categorization*	*T. categorization*	*P. categorization*	*M. categorization*	*T. categorization*
P. categorization						
M. categorization	* +16			+++ +48		
T. categorization	++++* +55	++++* +91		++++ +77	++++ +87	

	Total sample		
	P. categorization	*M. categorization*	*T. categorization*
P. categorization			
M. categorization	+++* +31		
T. categorization	++++* +66	++++ +88	

E

Cause (see Table 10.27)

Relationships between the physical and social uses of cause are all positive, though not all significant. Evidence of similarity between the two content-type uses of cause is greater than that of dissimilarity.

TABLE 10.27   *Cause related to cause*

	Girls				Boys			
	P. cause	*S. cause: Proximal*	*Distal*	*T. cause*	*P. cause*	*S. cause: Proximal*	*Distal*	*T. cause*
P. cause								
S. cause: Proximal	+09*				+28*			
Distal	+++* +40	+16			+12*	+09		
T. cause	++++* +83	+* +25	++++* +70		++++* +87	+++ +55	++ +36	

Total sample

	P. cause	*S. cause: Proximal*	*Distal*	*T. cause*
P. cause				
S. cause: Proximal	+++* +29			
Distal	+++* +28	+11†		
T. cause	++++* +86	++++*† +49	++++* +49	

Consequence (see Table 10.28)

The stronger relationships are between social and moral consequence. This is not surprising, since the content type of both questions is human, and the consequences are in the form of outcomes which are to be attained through the appropriate action or non-action by

TABLE 10.28 *Consequence related to consequence*

	Girls				Boys			
	P. consequence	*M. consequence*	*S. consequence*	*T. consequence*	*P. consequence*	*M. consequence*	*S. consequence*	*T. consequence*
P. consequence								
M. consequence	++ +30				+11			
S. consequence	* +16	++† +34			+10	++ +40		
T. consequence	++++* +60	+++++† +89	++++ +53		++ +37	++++ +89	++++ +60	

Total sample

	P. consequence	*M. consequence*	*S. consequence*	*T. consequence*
P. consequence				
M. consequence	++ +21			
S. consequence	+14	+++† +33		
T. consequence	++++* +48	+++†* +90	++++* +52	

human actors. Physical consequence is a different sort of answer. However, physical consequence does give positive relationships with both social and moral consequence. For boys the positive relationship between physical and moral consequence is probably due to a high proportion of negative, actor-oriented punishment responses contained in the total score for moral consequence, since this is the only subcategory which has a positive relationship with physical consequence ($r = +0.22$, not sig.), apart from all actor-oriented. This is not true for the girls.

For this mode too there is no evidence to suggest that there is a fundamental difference in meaning across the different content types.

2 *External relationships for the same mode of different content types*
Again there seems to be little point in an analysis of modes other than categorization, cause and consequence. The comparisons which can be made are as follows:

Categorization

The content types, physical and moral   with all other scoring categories for
                                                'why' questions

Cause

The content types, physical and social   with all other scoring categories for
                                                  'why' questions

Consequence

The content types, physical, moral and   with all other scoring categories for
social   'why' questions

Categorization

There is only one relationship which significantly separates the two content-type uses of categorization; for girls, moral categorization has a slight positive correlation with irrelevance ($r = +0.23, p < 0.10$) which is significantly different from that of physical categorization ($r = -0.20$, not sig.; z diff., $p < 0.05$). If we examine subcategories of moral categorization, we find that all have slight positive relationships, object categorization almost reaching significance ($r = +0.22$). For boys, although the majority of subcategories have slight negative correlations with irrelevance, object categorization is significantly positive ($r = +0.33, p < 0.10$). (This is further suggestive of its similarity to cause and consequence modes for the boys, since proximal cause is positively associated with irrelevance ($r = +0.40, p < 0.05$), and so is total consequence, though not significantly ($r = +0.24$, not sig.).)

The general picture overwhelmingly supports the similarity of the different uses of categorization.

Cause

There is only one relationship which separates either proximal social cause or distal social cause from physical cause; specified moral authority has, for boys, a more negative ($r = -0.22$, not sig.) relationship with proximal social cause than with physical cause ($r = +0.37$, $p < 0.05$; z diff., $p < 0.05$). However, the correlation between specified authority and distal cause ($r = +0.22$) suggests that a summed score for social cause would reduce this difference below significance.

Consequence (see Tables 10.29, 30 and 31)

Most of the differences between the separate-content type uses of consequence are in relation to the categorization mode. It is the

TABLE 10.29   *Consequence related to categorization*

	Girls			Boys		
	P. consequence	*M. consequence*	*S. consequence*	*P. consequence*	*M. consequence*	*S. consequence*
P. categorization	+13	+14	+21	* +14	++* −44	−08
M. categorization: Simple	+12	* −12	++* +28	+15	+ −35	+16
Object	+05	+11	+08	−20	+18	+20
Action	+17	+05	+++ +37	* +23	++* −40	+10
Person	−20	−01	−08	−05	+ −33	−29
All M. categorization	+10	+08	++ +34	+17	+ −35	+08
T. categorization	+14	+13	+++ +40	* +20	++* −38	+08

more negative relationships with the simple and action subcategories of moral categorization which differentiate moral from other content uses of consequence, particularly for the boys. If we break down moral consequence, we find that for the boys the positive subcategory behaves more like physical and social consequence in this relationship, and likewise with physical categorization. We could suggest that physical and social consequence share with moral positive consequence, as it is used by boys, the general categorical element we hypothesized earlier (p. 217).

TABLE 10.30 *The subcategories of consequence related to categorization*

	Boys						
	M. consequence: Positive	*Actor-oriented, punishment*	*Actor-oriented, other ill-effect*	*All actor-oriented*	*Action-oriented*	*Other-oriented*	*Negative general*
P. categorization	+04	+ −34	−03	++ −40	−07	−21	−16
M. categorization	* +13	−16	++* −40	++* −40	+11	−14	−18

Some of the differences between moral and social consequence in relation to categorization might be explained in terms of the small relevance that categorization has to the social questions. This would mean that subjects who gave longer answers to Q.21 tended to give a greater number of consequences and not categorizations, while those who gave longer answers to moral questions tended to give a greater number of either categorizations or consequences, but less likely both.

There exists, particularly for boys, a difference between the different content type uses of consequence as these are related to cause. This is understandable in the light of the smaller acceptability of an appeal to consequence for physical questions, particularly when these are man-centred, e.g. 'So that you can catch it' in reply to 'Why does a ball come down when you throw it up in the air?'

TABLE 10.31 *Consequence related to cause*

	Girls			Boys		
	P. consequence	*M. consequence*	*S. consequence*	*P. consequence*	*M. consequence*	*S. consequence*
S. cause: Proximal	+01	−02	+05	−25	+17	+17
Distal	+12	+++ +39	+16	−12	+30	+27
P. cause	* −19	+* +26	++* +32	+++* −48	+* +32	−02
T. cause	* −13	++* +30	++* +31	+* −32	++* +38	+09

Summary

Both 'internal' and 'external' relationships of the modes which we have examined are generally supportive of the similarity of the modes as they are applied to differing content types.

Certain of the subcategories of moral consequence are markedly more negative in their relationship with the simple and action subcategories of categorization than are physical and social consequence, particularly for boys. We do not know how much of a 'categorical' element as demonstrated by simple and action subcategories is present in physical and social consequence. Although cause and consequence may be grouped together as empirical modes (see the next section), yet when certain consequences are given as explanations for physical phenomena these may be considered less acceptable than causes.

We conclude that, in spite of the different ranges of acceptable modes which are available for answering questions of differing content types, the categorization, cause and consequence modes do appear to represent points of view which contain centrally stable elements, regardless of the content of the questions which they are used to answer.

(d) HIGHER-ORDER GROUPINGS OF MODES OF ANSWER FOR 'WHY' QUESTIONS

1 A basic dichotomy for ascribing 'focus' to modes of answer for 'why' questions

The nature of separation

Without looking further than the mode definitions themselves, we can make a logical division between a focus on the status of the proposition contained in the question and a focus on empirical data not mentioned in the question; the status of the proposition is accepted as given. Thus a restatement, e.g. 'Because it is', introduces no new empirical information, while an appeal to consequence, e.g. 'So that he will look nice and clean', relates the shaving mentioned in the question to information about the effect of shaving which has not already been given.

The ascription of foci to modes

Some modes fall into one category, some into another and some contain both foci. We can write out a table to show the distribution of modes according to focus. It will be noticed that subcategorizing may show up alternative possibilities for focus within the same mode. Further qualifications will be noted later (p. 246).

All subcategorizations given in the table are those which were actually scored, although not all those scored are included, and those which were scored at some point were not necessarily included in the final matrix. Certain subcategorizations which might have been made could have shown up other differences in focus within a mode. The focus ascribed to each mode in this table is that which is thought *more likely* to be associated with the mode.

Mode	Subcategory	Focus (I, propositional; II, empirical)	Function
1 Denial of oddity		I	States that the proposition is non-problematic
2 Restatement of question		I	States that the explanation of the proposition lies in the proposition itself

Mode	Subcategory	Focus (I, propositional II, empirical)	Function
3 Regularity		I	States whether the proposition is variant or invariant
4 Essence		I	States that the proposition is necessarily true because of the definition of part of it.
5 Authority	Unspecified	I or II	States that the proposition is necessarily true for some reason which may be logical or physical
	Specified	II	States that the injunction of some named authority or the operation of some general law results in the thesis taking place
6 Emotions or wishes	Actor's	I or II	May assume that particular emotions are a necessary or implied intervening variable, or may ascribe motive.
	Others'	II	The feelings of some other party are said to affect an event happening
7 Analogy		II	States that the thesis of the proposition has certain similarities with another different one
8 Categorization		I or II	States that, through an examination of its meaning or empirical correlates, the proposition or part of it can be included in a higher-order set. Further, ascription to the high-order set means that it has certain similar empirical features to those of other members of the set

Mode	Subcategory	Focus (I, propositional II, empirical)	Function
9 Cause		II	Specific events, attributes of objects or objects present, prior in time to the thesis, are said to be responsible for the thesis taking place
10 Consequence		II	Specific events subsequent in time to the thesis are said to have a determining effect upon it

Qualifications: the relevance of content and sequence

We mentioned earlier (p. 244) that the way in which we have actually scored our data may make the above separation rather incomplete. Mention of a season of the year (generally autumn or winter) in the answer to 'Why do the leaves fall off the trees?' was scored under 'regularity'. Nevertheless, as well as indicating that the proposition is not always true, such an answer supplies specific information, which may be of the same sort as that under 'categorization' in that it implies a connection with or a similarity to other events and features belonging to the same season. This variation in the 'regularity' mode could be called a variation along the specific-general dimension and again be paralleled by similar variations within the authority and categorization modes which are associated with differences in focus. A specified authority may in fact be almost so general as to be very similar to an unspecified authority. We have polarized answers rather than graded them along continuous dimensions.

Restatement of the question embraces a number of possible subcategories which were not in fact separated. One such separation which might have been made was that over whether any restatement which followed a probe was a restatement of the original question or of the probe. An example may help to show this difference:

> Q. Why shouldn't anyone steal?
> A. Because you get put into prison.
> Probe Q. Why do you get put into prison?
> A.1 Because you have been stealing.
> A.2 Because you shouldn't steal.

The last two answers (1 and 2) would be counted as restatement and they both repeat information contained in a previous question rather than that in the probe question immediately preceding the answer. The following answer (3) repeats information contained in the immediately preceding probe.

A.3 Because you do.

It too is a restatement.

The first two were scored as restatements, *not* on the basis of their focus (which had not yet been discovered), but because they failed to supply any new information in the context of the total answer. If restatement were scored on the basis of focus the answer could be considered a causal one.

Within the emotions mode we failed to make a separation between those wants directed to the thesis of the question and those directed upon some consequence. The former would be more closely associated with focus on the proposition, the latter with focus on empirical data. An example of the difference is as follows:

Q. Why should children do what their parents tell them to?
A.1 Because they want to.
A.2 Because they want to grow up properly.

Both of these answers are actor-oriented. The former expresses a particular relationship between 'want' and 'ought' and the second signifies a motive to achieve some purpose with normatively testable content.

Further implications of a difference in focus

Without saying that either focus is better than the other, we may uncover some of the implications involved in these two broadly separable ways of answering.

One important implication is related to the different possibilities for variation in content allowed by the different foci. When we know that a particular focus on the proposition mode has been used, we have a good idea as to what the exact content of the answer will be, whereas when we know that one of the foci on empirical data mode has been used we are less likely to be able to predict this content.

For instance, if we are simply told that a person has answered a question in a causal mode, then we know that he has brought to bear on the problem empirical information about events objects or attributes present prior to the thesis and said to be responsible for its occurrence. We do not know the precise nature of the information. It may establish a connection that we did not realize existed. Nor, if we are told that the answer is in the categorization mode, do we know which category was used for which component of the proposition. However, if somebody has made an appeal to essence, then we are aware that he has made the truth of the whole proposition contained in the question a function of the connotation of one of the words or phrases of the proposition; the possibilities are limited. As is the case for categorization, we do not know exactly which component has been selected but, whichever part is selected, we know *how* it will be related to the rest, i.e. tautologically (even though this may rest upon an *ad hoc* stipulated definition rather than a generally accepted one).

From the point of view of the answerer, the two different foci make different types of demands upon him. When he chooses to focus upon the proposition, he needs to have only a limited number of sentence frames available into which he can fit an answer to a question regardless of its specific semantic features. However, if he focuses upon empirical problems, such as cause and consequence, he is obliged to reply with particular facts which are related to the content of the question.

The modes which focus on the proposition are less likely to contain information which can be shown to be false (unless one chooses to call all such responses failures to answer the question posed). They are relatively 'safe' answers from this point of view, while those which introduce new empirical propositions are empirically testable and may be found to be false in whole or in part.

2 The evidence relating to the construct validity of the dichotomy of focus (see Tables 10.32, 33, 34 and 35) Supportive evidence that such a separation corresponds to real differences in answering dispositions would roughly show that cause, particularly distal cause, and consequence modes associate positively together as focus on empirical data modes, and so should restatement, regularity (particularly regularity alone) and perhaps unspecified authority associate positively together as focus on the proposition of the question modes. There should also be some evidence of a negative relationship between the two groups of modes. Categorization might be expected to fall between the two. We do not know enough about how the emotions mode was used to predict how it would fit in.

In Tables 10.32, 33 and 34 we take those categories which seem to represent the more extreme cases of the two answering dispositions and see how they relate among themselves and across foci.

Table 10.32 shows that although all relationships between focus on the proposition modes are positive, that between unspecified authority and regularity alone is negligible in size.

TABLE 10.32   *Focus on proposition of the question modes*

	Girls			Boys		
	T. restatement	*Q.23, R.1, regularity: alone*	*M. authority: unspecified*	*T. restatement*	*Q.23, R.1, regularity: alone*	*M. authority: unspecified*
T. restatement						
Q.23, R.1 regularity: alone	+06			+ +34		
M. authority: unspecified	++ +30	+02		+18	+02	

Relationships between the cause and consequence modes are with one exception positive.

The tendency of unspecified authority to relate positively with the causal mode, however, is evidence against the separation, and so is the slight positive non-significant relationship between restatement and cause and consequence modes.

Boys and girls seem to differ with regard to the categorization mode. For boys, categorization tends to relate positively with focus on the proposition modes and more negatively with focus on empirical data modes. The only significant negative relationships are with moral consequence. For girls it has virtually no relationship with focus on the proposition modes and is more positively related to focus on empirical data modes. The only significant relationship is with social consequence.

The way that the categorization mode diverges for the boys is in itself evidence in support of the dichotomy. Why it does so might have something to do with the particular content of the categorizations; that it is more propositional than empirical.

It may be something to do with the age of the subjects that there is not a stronger distinction between the two foci such as to give rise to consistent answering according to focus. What might be particularly relevant to age is a notion of the necessity of events or actions

TABLE 10.33 *Focus on empirical data modes*

	Girls				Boys			
	P. cause	*S. cause: distal*	*M. consequence*	*S. consequence*	*P. cause*	*S. cause: distal*	*M. consequence*	*S. consequence*
P. cause								
S. cause: distal	+++ +40				+12			
M. consequence	+ +26	+++ +39			+ +32	+30		
S. consequence	++ +32	+16	++ +34		−02	+27	++ +40	

TABLE 10.34 *Focus on proposition of the question modes related to focus on empirical data modes*

	Girls			Boys		
	T. restatement	*Q23 R1 regularity: alone*	*M. authority: unspecified*	*T. restatement*	*Q23 R1 regularity: alone*	*M. authority: unspecified*
P. cause	+15	+ −23	+ +23	−23	−22	−17
S. cause: distal	+01	−18	++ +27	−17	−11	+28
M. consequence	+19	++ −32	+03	−09	−22	−05
S. consequence	+07	+ −24	−02	+03	++ −42	+13

TABLE 10.35 *Focus on proposition of the question modes and focus on empirical data modes related to categorization*

	Girls		Boys	
	P. categorization	*M. categorization*	*P. categorization*	*M. categorization*
T. restatement	+01	+03	+* +32	+* +32
Q23 R1 regularity: alone	00	−01	* +19	−13
M. authority: unspecified	00	00	* +23	+* +32
P. cause	−01	+20	−20	+06
S. cause: distal	−06	+20	−11	−03
M. consequence	+14	+08	++* −44	+* −35
S. consequence	+21	++ +34	−08	+08

which is implied by the use of the authority mode by children who also give empirical reasons. This may spring from their limited experience of alternatives and their own relatively powerless position with regard to others. (More information relevant to this may be found in Kohlberg's (1969) elaboration of Piaget's (1932) ideas about moral judgment.)

3 *Cause and effect* Although the foci on the proposition of the question modes do not all associate positively together, foci on empirical data modes do, and these could alternatively be described as forming a cause-effect group of modes.

The data point to no other basis for grouping modes together into higher-order categories.

(iv) An examination of modes of answer for 'non-why' and 'why' questions

(a) *INTRODUCTION*

Our mode analysis for answers to 'non-why' questions is very limited in terms of the range of different modes. As far as answers to 'when' and 'where' questions are concerned, we separate what we consider is a more objective mode from a group of more relative ones. We also separate out the mode relative to own age for answering one question (Q.11), since it may be the most normatively acceptable way of answering that particular question. For one 'who' question there is a person-specification mode of answer and there is a functional definition mode for answers to 'What is a school?'

It seems to be most convenient to deal first with how modes of answer to 'when' and 'where' questions relate to modes of answer to 'why' questions and then with how the person specification and functional definition modes do.

(b) MODES OF ANSWER FOR 'WHEN' AND 'WHERE' QUESTIONS RELATED TO MODES OF ANSWER FOR 'WHY' QUESTIONS (see Tables 10.36 and 37)

When we relate modes for answering 'when' and 'where' questions to those for answering 'why' questions broken down according to the tentative separations based upon the dichotomy of focus, we find that the groups which seem to have the strongest relationship are the

TABLE 10.36 *'When' and 'where' mode 1 related to 'why' categorization*

	Girls			Boys		
	P. categorization	*M. categorization*	*T. categorization*	*P. categorization*	*M. categorization*	*T. categorization*
Q.1, mode 1	+13	++ +31	++ +31	+ +31	+26	+ +31
Q.18, mode 1*a*	+ +23	++++ +44	++++ +47	+13	−06	00
Q.2, mode 1	+ +23	+ +23	++ +29	+17	+10	+14
Q.4, mode 1+	+20	++ +28	++ +33	−05	−14	−17
Q.6, mode 1+	++ +28	−03	+08	+06	−03	+06

objective modes 1 and 1+ for both 'when' and 'where' questions and the different content uses of categorization as these are used by the girls. The relationships for the boys are confined to that between physical and total categorization and the use of mode 1 for Q.1. Examination of the relationships of subcategories of moral categorization with these mode 1 categories shows that for girls each of the subcategories has a similar pattern of relationships to that of the others. For boys the object subcategory is significantly different from the simple and action subcategories in its positive relationships with the use of mode 1a for answering Q.18.

TABLE 10.37 *The subcategories of categorization related to 'when' and 'where' mode 1*

	Girls				Boys			
	M. categorization: Simple	*Object*	*Action*	*Person*	*M. categorization: Simple*	*Object*	*Action*	*Person*
Q. 1, mode 1	+17	−07	++ +33	+07	+09	+27	+16	−08
Q. 18, mode 1a	+22	+20	++ +28	++ +28	* −26	++* +37	* −19	−12
Q. 2, mode 1	+19	+15	+11	+20	+09	+01	+16	+03
Q. 4, mode 1+	+20	+06	+ +25	+07	−15	−07	−15	+15
Q. 6, mode 1+	00	−06	+01	−07	−09	+21	−03	−19

Relationships of what we have termed the focus on the proposition of question mode with 'non-why' modes are generally negligible. For girls, specified authority relates positively to mode 3 for Q.11 ($r = +0.24$, $p < 0.10$) while total authority relates positively to mode 1+for Q.4 ($r = +0.29$, $p < 0.05$).

Among the relationships of focus on empirical data modes with modes for answering 'when' and 'where' questions there are very few significant ones. If we relate the six independent cause and consequence modes to the 'acceptable' modes (i.e. mainly 1 or 1+, but 3 for Q.11) for answering 'when' and 'where' questions, out of thirty-

F

six correlations the girls give only five negative ones, none of which approaches significance. However, the only significant positive relationship is between physical consequence and the precise form of mode 1 for Q.18 ($r = +0.33$, $p < 0.05$). For the boys, half the relationships are positive, half negative, while none is significant.

Although the boys have shown more consistent mode choices for 'when' and 'where' questions (see p. 202), the girls show a strong relationship between the use of mode 1 or 1+ and that of the categorization mode for both physical and moral questions. Relationships between mode 1 and other 'why' modes are generally nonsignificant. What is it that brings about this relationship between categorization and the more objective modes? Both might be described as relatively short, simple, objective and quite possibly learned sequences. They both appeal to stable and static rather than dynamic events. The failure for there to be significant relationships between categorization and the use of mode 3 implies that it is not simply the acceptability aspect which is relevant. Furthermore, the relationships with categorization of mode 1 answers to 'when' and 'where' questions is not simply a function of their being closely related together, since, particularly for girls, they are rather loosely related. The relationship with categorization seems to extract some common factor of the mode 1 answers.

(c) UNIQUE-PERSON SPECIFICATION RELATED TO MODES OF ANSWER FOR 'WHY' QUESTIONS

The only significant relationship between unique-person specification in answer to Q.9 and answering modes for 'why' questions for boys is that with social consequence ($r = +0.34$, $p < 0.10$). For girls there is a positive relationship with unspecified moral authority ($r = +0.23$, $p < 0.10$), while moral categorization just fails to give a significant negative relationship ($r = -0.22$, not sig.). There seem to be no grounds for including this category within any cross-question-type higher-order grouping.

(d) FUNCTIONAL DEFINITION RELATED TO MODES OF ANSWER FOR 'WHY' QUESTIONS

For the girls almost all relationships between the functional definition of school mode and modes of answer for 'why' questions are positive, and nine are significant. There is a significant negative relationship with regularity alone ($r = -0.24$, $p < 0.10$), however, and this is the only negative relationship except for that with total regularity ($r = -0.08$).

It seems most likely that the relationships are artefactual, and that the positive relationships say more about the relative likelihood of supplying answers of any length rather than about common or complementary aspects of their content. This is borne out by the high negative correlation between a functional definition and N.A. ($r = -0.44$, $p < 0.001$). For boys, relationships with categorization and physical consequence are slightly negative, likewise with physical consequence, but otherwise they resemble the girls, although only the relationship with restatement reaches significance ($r = +0.32$, $p < 0.10$). For boys there is a negative association with D.K. ($r = -0.35$, $p < 0.10$) rather than with N.A.

(e) SUMMARY AND CONCLUSIONS

Although it is for the boys that we find more coherent relationships among uses of mode 1 and among what we have called 'acceptable' modes for answering 'when' and 'where' questions, it is for the girls that these modes unite together in sharing similar external relationships with modes for answering 'why' questions.

Thus modes 1 and 1+, as they are used for 'when' and 'where' questions, have significant positive relationships with the categorization mode for 'why' questions. The acceptable modes, which consist of the same group, but with the addition of mode 3 for Q.11, tend to have weak though positive relationships with the cause-effect modes. It may be that common formal or contextual features required or frequently used for the expression of these modes of answer are responsible for the positive connection between the groups. A following section (3) of this chapter attempts to sort out such possibilities. There may, however, be explanations of a semantic kind and it is our responsibility to consider such in this section.

The categorization mode is usually concerned with stable, static features of an item or a situation. It ascribes an attribute or a label to a participant or event. In contrast with cause or consequence modes, it does not seek to work out changing relationships between participants in a dynamic situation. The objective mode 1 shares this more static point of view. Alternative responses to 'when' and 'where' questions would seek more to relate an event or place to a unique or even shifting reference-point rather than to an objective fixed time-place scale. At the same time the objective reference is the more acceptable, given the situation in which the answers were made. Categorization responses are fairly acceptable, normatively, although the cause-effect modes could be considered more likely to have the greater explanatory power and for this reason to be more acceptable than categorizations.

These two factors, 'acceptability' and 'static-dynamic', might both be operative in the decision to answer with mode 1 to 'when' and 'where' questions. For the girls, it looks as though the pressure towards a safe static reference is predominant among those who answer with modes 1 or 1+. It may be, as we suggest later (see p. 275), that although boys give a significantly greater number of causal explanations, yet these are of a less demanding and less forceful kind. This might account for the failure to find a relationship between the group of acceptable 'non-why' modes and cause-effect modes for boys. Such a relationship might be found if we could isolate out the 'better quality' cause-effect answers in some way. If this is true, it leads us to suggest that, for the boys, the acceptability factor is dominant over the static-dynamic in answering 'when' and 'where' questions. The relationships, for boys, between mode 1 and 1+ and mode 3 for Q.11 (see Table 10.4) gave rise to the notion of an acceptability factor in the first place, and the relationship between mode 1 and categorization (see Table 10.36) is far less convincing for the boys than it is for the girls.

In conclusion, the relationships among modes for 'non-why' and 'why' lead us to think, but rather tentatively in the absence of significant correlations, that an acceptability factor, which constituted the only higher-order basis on which 'non-why' modes were grouped, may be operative for the selection of 'why' modes as well as for 'when' and 'where' modes. Another group of modes comprising mode 1 for answers to 'when' and 'where' questions and categorization for answers to both physical and moral 'why' questions might cohere together on the basis of a more static than dynamic point of view.

2　Formal and contextual features of 'non-why' answers

(i) Introduction

Not all the possible formal and contextual features mentioned in Chapters 2 and 3 were in fact scored. Those which were are mentioned below under the relevant divisions of answer area, linguistic level, aspect, as well as certain additional features.

(a) ANSWER AREA

The only separation made according to 'answer area' apart from that occurring under 'presupposition', was within grammatical inappropriateness. This initially supplied three categories: (1) grammatical inappropriateness, concerned with the area of answer *as* answer (2) question-answer discord, dealing with systemic parallels between question and answer, and (3) intra-answer discord and grammatical mistakes containing any other mistakes not covered in the first two areas. Since discordant answers were rare, the last two ((2) and (3)) were collapsed under the heading 'grammatical mistakes'. The results are reported under (ii) levels and (iii) aspects.

(b) LINGUISTIC LEVELS

The three levels, grammar, lexis and context, were all applied in the way described in Chapters 2 and 3.

(c) ASPECT OF ANSWER

The three aspects of appropriateness, completeness and presupposition described in Chapters 2 and 3 were all included at all levels, except for contextual presupposition, about which our data gave no direct information. Lexical presupposition was scored by the number of items exhibiting it, and grammatical presupposition as maximal, minimal or intermediate. For appropriateness and completeness the aspects were scored as the number of instances of inappropriateness and incompleteness, apart from contextual completeness, for which a count of the information items mentioned was made: the more different and accurate items given, the more complete the answer. To facilitate comparison with the other scores, we have reversed this item to contextual incompleteness.

The only additional categories within aspects (as these were originally conceived) which were finally included in the matrix are related to lexical incompleteness and were grouped together under the heading 'vague lexis'. Items counted for this were of three sorts: the nominal group general substitute 'thing' for non-human nouns; pronouns without previous or subsequent reference to nouns; verbal group substitutes, such as 'do'. Lexical incompleteness included all other instances of lack of specificity, including those phrases which contribute little more than noise to an utterance, or point to a lack of exactness in the accompanying speech, like 'and all that' 'sort of thing' or which depend entirely upon extra-linguistic indicators to signal their meaning, e.g. 'About that tall' or 'I live down there'. Previous work led us to think that vague lexis might differ functionally from lexical incompleteness in that it might be a means whereby information may be generalized and simplified, or whereby a lack of knowledge of a specific linguistic item may be overcome by the use of such general expressions which are further qualified by the use of other known items. However, in given instances the two categories may function similarly.

It seemed appropriate to count certain features which were not specified in the original schedule. One of these is the aspect *substitution* which has both lexical and grammatical counterparts, but was only rarely used. Grammatical substitution was in fact scored for only one type of question, viz. the 'how' (mode 2—compound) type 'How well . . . ?' and 'How tall . . . ?'. For grammatical substitution to be scored, the answer had to borrow a different form from that suggested by the question but which was semantically equivalent. Lexical substitution was scored for the same questions when lexical items of the question were substituted for by different ones in the answer. Lexical substitution was only scored in structures where there was no grammatical substitution. Again semantic equivalence (a somewhat difficult judgment) was required, and if this was not clear the item was only scored as lexically inappropriate.

(d) *ADDITIONAL FEATURES*

Additional features counted were the incidence of the misuse of the prepositions 'up' and 'down' (which was not counted separately under inappropriateness of any sort), the use of the preposition 'round', any mention of the name of the sweet-shop in the answer to 'Where is your favourite sweet-shop?', and the failure to give a proper noun, referring to a street, town, or shop, in answer to a 'where' question.

The relationships between these features are examined in the following order:

> Relationships within linguistic levels.
> Relationships within aspects of answer.
> Relationships between levels and aspects.

(ii) **Relationships within linguistic levels**

(a) *GRAMMATICAL*

Within the level of grammar there does not seem to be a definite indication of a disposition towards generally inadequate use of grammar showing up across the different scoring categories, inappropriateness, mistakes, incompleteness, presupposition. For boys and girls together, and particularly for boys, grammatical inappropriateness is associated with other grammatical mistakes, suggesting that answering behaviour is not demanding grammatical skills peculiar to itself, but is simply one area among others in which a child given to making mistakes in grammar will make them.

TABLE 10.38 *Relationships at the level of grammar*

	Girls				Boys			
	Grammatical inappropriateness	*Grammatical mistakes*	*Grammatical incompleteness*	*Grammatical < max. presupposition*	*Grammatical inappropriateness*	*Grammatical mistakes*	*Grammatical incompleteness*	*Grammatical < max. presupposition*
Grammatical Inappropriateness								
Grammatical mistakes	+17				+ +35			
Grammatical incompleteness	+05	+++ +37			+07	−01		
Grammatical < max. presupposition	−02	−01	++ −27		−12	+04	++ −43	

TABLE 10.39 *Relationships at the level of lexis*

	Girls				Boys			
	Lexical inappropriateness	*Lexical incompleteness*	*Vague lexis*	*Lexical presupposition*	*Lexical inappropriateness*	*Lexical incompleteness*	*Vague lexis*	*Lexical presupposition*
lexical inappropriateness								
lexical incompleteness	+++ +43				−01			
vague lexis	+++ +40	+++ +42			+12	+09		
lexical presupposition	+04	+ +23	+ +23		−03	−14	+15	

(b) LEXICAL

At the level of lexis the boys and girls diverge. For girls the different lexical categories are associated positively, so that those who use inappropriate lexical items tend also to use lexically incomplete and vague expressions. Furthermore, incompleteness and vagueness are associated with one another. Boys show a weak relationship between lexical inappropriateness and lexical substitution, which is also true for girls, and might suggest an inattention to or an unawareness of differences between words. When boys and girls are put together, the relation between incompleteness and inappropriateness remains at the same level of significance as for girls alone, while the other ones, involving vague lexis, remain significant, but are reduced. We may be able to regard these measures as independent assessments of the same thing, but it will be necessary first to examine their external relationships.

(c) CONTEXTUAL

At the level of context, for the total sample, contextual inappropriateness is positively correlated with contextual incompleteness ($r = +0.20$, $p < 0.10$), suggesting that subjects who give untrue information do *not* do so in the context of a relatively large amount of true information.

(iii) Relationships within aspects of answers

(a) APPROPRIATENESS

An attempt to discover some validity for an appropriateness category might be successful, since grammatical mistakes and lexical inappropriateness (the latter covering all three answer areas, the former two of them) occur together for girls and for the total sample. Grammatical inappropriateness does not correlate significantly with lexical inappropriateness, although this may be partly due to its relative scarcity.

(b) COMPLETENESS

Grammatical and lexical incompleteness do not co-occur. Contextual incompleteness is negatively related to vague lexis for boys alone and for boys and girls together, which is quite likely to mean nothing more than that, within the longer descriptions of processes, the use of the general markers making up vague lexis is more likely to occur.

TABLE 10.40 *Relationships within the aspect inappropriateness*

	Girls				Boys			
	Grammatical inappropriateness	Grammatical mistakes	Lexical inappropriateness	Contextual inappropriateness	Grammatical inappropriateness	Grammatical mistakes	Lexical inappropriateness	Contextual inappropriateness
Grammatical inappropriateness								
Grammatical mistakes	+17				+ +35			
Lexical inappropriateness	−10	++++ +44			−15	00		
Contextual inappropriateness	+01	−22	−06		−09	+05	+10	

The girls show a negative correlation between contextual incompleteness and grammatical incompleteness which may also be related to the difficulty of giving a coherent description of a process.

(c) PRESUPPOSITION

Relationships between presupposition at the lexical and grammatical levels are somewhat necessary since lexical presupposition cannot occur in a maximally presuppositive answer.

(d) SUBSTITUTION

For neither girls nor boys do the different levels of substitution show any relationship with one another. Positive relationships might anyhow be reduced by the prohibition which does not allow lexical substitution to be counted in structures which are themselves grammatical substitutions.

(iv) Relationships between levels and aspects

We have now observed the patterns of relationship of the various aspects at the different levels and of the three levels within aspects. There are further correlations between an aspect at one level and a different aspect at a different level. For the girls of the sample, grammatical mistakes and lexical presupposition give results. Grammatical mistakes have two positive relationships, one with lexical incompleteness ($r = +0.44$, $p < 0.001$) and one with vague lexis which is a type of lexical incompleteness ($r = +0.40$, $p < 0.01$). Lexical presupposition is negatively correlated with grammatical inappropriateness ($r = -0.27$, $p < 0.05$) and almost achieves a significant negative correlation with grammatical incompleteness ($r = -0.22$, not sig.).

The boys, like the girls, show a positive correlation between grammatical mistakes and vague lexis ($r = +0.52$, $p < 0.01$) and also a non-significant positive one between grammatical mistakes and lexical presupposition ($r = +0.30$, not sig.). The total sample yields a negative relationship between grammatical mistakes and contextual incompleteness.

(v) Relationships among additional features

The supplying of the name of the sweet-shop seems to be negatively related to the indication of non-specificity and slight inaccuracy suggested by the use of 'round' and 'up' and 'down'. For boys the

TABLE 10.41   *Relationships among non-aspect items*

	Girls				Boys			
	Q.6, name of sweet-shop	*Where, misuse of 'up' and 'down'*	*Where, use of 'round'*	*Where, no proper name of place*	*Q.6, name of sweet-shop*	*Where, misuse of 'up' and 'down'*	*Where, use of 'round'*	*Where, no proper name of place*
Q. 6, name of sweet-shop								
Where, misuse of 'up' and 'down'	+ −26				−20			
Where use of 'round'	−22	−13			+ −35	++ +41		
Where, no proper name of place	+11	+19	+03		−26	+ +33	+++ +51	

use of 'round' is associated with a misuse of 'up' and 'down', and both are connected with answers which do not supply a proper name of place.

(vi) Relationships between additional features and aspects of answer

The positive relationship between grammatical inappropriateness and giving the name of the sweet-shop for girls ($r = +0.29$, $p < 0.05$) may indicate that the name of the sweet-shop was all that was given (i.e. rather than its location).

Lexical inappropriateness correlates positively with the misuse of 'up' and 'down' for girls ($r = +0.25$, $p < 0.10$) and almost for boys ($r = +0.28$, not sig.). The colloquial use of these prepositions was thought to be too mild a case of inappropriateness to be included in that category, but these associations suggest that it might have been sensible to include them after all.

There are several relationships with incompleteness categories.

TABLE 10.42   *Non-aspect items related to incompleteness*

	Girls				Boys			
	Q.6, name of sweet-shop	*Where, misuse of 'up' and 'down'*	*Where, use of 'round'*	*Where, no proper name of place*	*Q.6, name of sweet-shop*	*Where, misuse of 'up' and 'down'*	*Where, use of 'round'*	*Where, no proper name of place*
Grammatical incompleteness	+09	−08	+09	−07	++ +45	−09	+ −35	++ −42
Lexical incompleteness	−18	+++ +36	+12	++ +27	−16	++++ +60	+++ +54	++++ +66
vague lexis	−05	+14	−06	−07	+27	+13	−08	−01
Contextual incompleteness	+11	−05	+03	+++ +38	+05	−14	+17	+18

The positive association of the three categories representing imprecision with lexical incompleteness might suggest that it is in the vague answers to 'where' questions that lexical incompleteness chiefly occurs, especially since there is no consistent negative relationship with contextual incompleteness. Mode relationships with lexical completeness bear out this suggestion (see p. 268). There is a suggestion that grammatical incompleteness is not a consequence of lack of specificity, but is associated with the category which gives some very specific although unasked-for information, viz. the name of a sweet-shop.

These non-aspect categories are, for the boys, heavily dependent upon choices of answer mode for 'where' questions. There seems

TABLE 10.43 *Non-aspect items related to 'where' modes*

	Girls				Boys			
	Q.6, name of sweet-shop	Where, misuse of 'up' and 'down'	Where, use of 'round'	Where, no proper name of place	Q.6, name of sweet-shop	Where, misuse of 'up' and 'down'	Where, use of 'round'	Where, no proper name of place
Q. 2, mode 1	−08	+06	−01	+++ −40	+ +32	−20	−21	++++ −70
Q. 4, mode 1+	+06	−15	−08	+++ −40	++ +22	++++ −39	−68	+++ −52
Q. 6, mode 1+	+++ −38	−11	+17	++++ −51	++ −36	−09	−22	−22

little point in discussing them apart from the modes of answer with which they occur.

(vii) Summary and conclusions

What emerges is a coherent group of categories consisting of the aspects inappropriateness and incompleteness at the three levels, each related to a greater or lesser degree with the total group in a fairly consistent way for both sexes, but without demonstrating a strikingly clear pattern.

The substitution categories are not included in the summary sub-matrix because they did not relate in similar ways for both boys and girls. Thus it is difficult at present to understand what is involved in making such responses. The presupposition categories are not included because they are not independent of each other. Part of the negative relationship which contextual incompleteness has with other categories may result from a failure to control for 'amount of speech' to which it is surely related. We have some evidence for the existence of independent factors corresponding to the levels of grammar, lexis and context, while that relevant to the aspects of inappropriateness and incompleteness is less supportive. This evidence receives further attention in Chapter 11.

TABLE 10.44 *Relationships between the aspects inappropriateness and incompleteness at the levels of grammar, lexis and context*

	Total sample							
	Grammatical inappropriateness	Grammatical mistakes	Lexical inappropriateness	Contextual inappropriateness	Grammatical incompleteness	Lexical incompleteness	Vague lexis	Contextual incompleteness
Grammatical inappropriateness								
Grammatical mistakes	++ +25							
Lexical inappropriateness	−15	++ +25						
Contextual inappropriateness	−01	−11	−01					
Grammatical incompleteness	+07	+ +18	++ +21	+02				
Lexical incompleteness	−05	++ +25	++ +26	−07	−15			
Vague lexis	00	++++ +47	++ +22	−09	+08	++ +23		
Contextual incompleteness	+11	+ −20	−02	+ +20	−10	00	++++ −38	

3   The relationship between formal and contextual features and the selection of answer modes for 'non-why' and 'why' questions

(i) Introduction

Through relating modes to features of form and context, we hope, as well as gaining indirect information about the validity of the analysis scheme, to discover something about the connection between ways of looking at a problem and those features which are characteristic of the verbal expression of such thought. We also hope to find out whether the selection of some modes rather than others is associated with the production of accurate statements about the world. For example, are modes which focus on empirical data characteristic of answerers who give contextually appropriate or contextually inappropriate information in other answering situations? Does the tendency to give what we have tentatively called more 'acceptable' modes to 'when' and 'where' questions go with a tendency to adhere to 'acceptable' standards at the level of grammar, lexis and context? Where this is *not* so, is it because there is a cost involved, such that acceptability at one level means less likelihood of acceptability at other levels?

We shall first examine relationships between the formal and contextual features and modes for 'non-why' questions. The 'non-why' modes will be discussed in three sections: those for 'when' and 'where', the unique specification for 'who' and the functional definition for what a school is (Q.10). For each section there will be an examination of relationships with the aspects of appropriateness, completeness, presupposition and substitution at the relevant levels. The decision to divide the examination according to aspects is simply one of convenience. Since we do not have evidence of a clear separation between aspects (p. 265), we shall postpone a discussion of aspect relationships with modes until all have been looked at. Relationships of modes of answer for 'why' questions with these same aspects will be examined in three sections, according to the earlier separation on the basis of focus. This will enable us, right at the outset, to separate off categorization, which was found to have particularly close links with the use of mode 1 and 1+ for answers to 'when' and 'where' questions. The three sections for 'why' questions then will be: categorization, focus on the proposition of the question modes, and focus on empirical data modes.

Finally, we shall seek to extract a total picture of which features or groups of features associate with which modes or groups of modes for both 'why' and 'non-why' questions.

(ii) Relationships between modes of answer and features of form and context for 'non-why' questions

(a) MODES USED FOR ANSWERS TO 'WHEN' AND 'WHERE' QUESTIONS

1 *Inappropriateness (see Table 10.45)* For girls, contextual inappropriateness is related positively to the use of mode 1+ for answers to Q.4, but negatively with mode 3 for Q.11. The positive relationship between grammatical mistakes and the precise use of mode 1 for

TABLE 10.45 *Acceptable 'when' and 'where' modes related to inappropriateness*

	Girls				Boys			
	Grammatical inappropriateness	Grammatical mistakes	Lexical inappropriateness	Contextual inappropriateness	Grammatical inappropriateness	Grammatical mistakes	Lexical inappropriateness	Contextual inappropriateness
Q. 1, mode 1	+10	+07	−13	+16	−22	−20	−04	+ −32
Q.11, mode 3	00	+ +23	+12	++ −28	+17	−09	−29	−07
Q. 18, mode 1*a*	+17	+22	−13	+05	+ −33	−08	−11	−11
Q. 2, mode 1	−12	+04	+03	+04	+16	+13	+01	+09
Q. 4, mode 1+	00	−21	−18	++ +31	00	−08	−06	+12
Q. 6, mode 1+	−10	++ −30	−21	+05	−19	++ −40	−29	+ −31

answers to Q.18 almost reaches significance. For boys, the 'acceptable' mode of answer for Q.6 yields significant negative correlations with inappropriateness categories.

2 *Incompleteness (see Table 10.46)* The negative relationship between lexical incompleteness and modes 1 and 1+ for answers of both girls and boys to Q.2 and Q.4 might imply that lexical incompleteness was particularly characteristic of answers which were of a more relative sort. For boys, vague lexis, which is a sort of lexical incompleteness, relates in the opposite way to the mode 1 answers to 'when' questions.

The use of acceptable modes for answering 'when' and 'where' questions is positively associated with the amount of information supplied about how to ride a bicycle or where the water in the tap comes from (contextual completeness), although the two mode 1+ answers for girls are significantly different from one another in their association with contextual completeness (z diff., $p < 0.05$).

TABLE 10.46 *Acceptable 'when' and 'where' modes related to incompleteness*

	Girls				Boys			
	Grammatical incompleteness	Lexical incompleteness	vague lexis	Contextual incompleteness	Grammatical incompleteness	Lexical incompleteness	Vague lexis	Contextual incompleteness
Q.1, mode 1	−07	−10	−02	00	+11	+12	+29	+ −34
Q.11, mode 3	−03	+18	+17	−18	+30	−26	+16	++ −46
Q.18, mode 1a	+10	+15	+04	+06	−03	00	+ +34	++ −40
Q. 2, mode 1	+15	+03	00	−18	+ +32	++ −43	+10	−17
Q. 4, mode 1+	−08	++ −31	−08	+12	++ +36	+++ −52	+09	−21
Q. 6, mode 1+	+09	+++ −42	+06	+++ −40	−29	++ −38	−16	−12

3 *Presupposition* There is some indication that for the boys the use of mode 1 in response to 'when' questions is associated with the more efficient way of answering, i.e. with maximal presupposition (Q.1, mode 1, $r = -0.38$, $p < 0.05$; Q.18, mode 1a, $r = -0.14$, not sig.).

4 *Substitution* There is only one significant correlation with substitution. That is a negative relationship between mode 1 answers for Q.2 and grammatical substitution ($r = -0.33$ $p < 0.10$).

Summary

It seems that acceptability in the area of modes of answering 'when' and 'where' questions is associated with acceptability in terms of grammatical, lexical and contextual aspects of appropriateness and completeness. However, this is not true for grammatical incompleteness, which may sometimes be regarded as a tendency to be *over*-precise in the use of structures (i.e. omitting elements), nor is it true for vague lexis, whose ambivalence we have noted previously (p. 257). There is minimal evidence of an association of the use of mode 1 with the more efficient maximal presupposition. The use of substitution does not seem to be a feature which is associated with acceptability of mode.

(b) UNIQUE-PERSON SPECIFICATION FOR 'WHO' (Q.9)

There are three formal and contextual features which have significant relationships with unique-person specification—namely, grammatical mistakes ($r = +0.36$, $p < 0.05$), contextual incompleteness ($r = -0.36, p < 0.05$) for boys, and grammatical substitution, which seems to function differently for boys and girls (girls, $r = +0.35$, $p < 0.01$; boys, $r = -0.38, p < 0.05$).

It may be that in this context the reason behind giving a unique-person specification of the teacher rather than her role is part of a general tendency to try to give information, even though this may involve making grammatical mistakes. We cannot make sense out of the divergent relationships with substitution.

(c) FUNCTIONAL DEFINITION FOR SCHOOL (Q.10)

We have already noted some artefactual relationships associated with functional definition (see p. 255). Here we find a negative relationship with contextual incompleteness (girls, $r = -0.35$, $p < 0.01$; boys, $r = -0.23$, not sig.) and a positive relationship with grammatical incompleteness for girls ($r = +0.26$, $p < 0.10$). Relationships with other incompleteness and with inappropriateness categories are rather more positive than negative, though not significantly so.

Such relationships may again be a function of a willingness and capacity to give information at all, together with the attendant deficiencies whch could not occur in the absence of verbal output.

(iii) Relationships between modes of answer for 'why' questions and features of form and context for 'non-why' questions

(a) CATEGORIZATION (see Tables 10.47, 48 and 49)

For categorization there are significant negative relationships with lexical inappropriateness, and with less than maximal grammatical presupposition. Hardly any other relationships even approach significance except for those with lexical presupposition, and that is likely to be a function of the direct dependence of lexical presupposition on the occurrence of less than maximal grammatical presupposition.

G

TABLE 10.47 *Categorization related to lexical inappropriateness and grammatical presupposition*

	Girls		Boys	
	Lexical inappropriateness	*Grammatical ∨ max. presupposition*	*Lexical inappropriateness*	*Grammatical ∨ max. presupposition*
P. categorization	+ −24	++ −33	+ −35	+ −32
M. categorization	+08	−06	+ −31	−17

Categorization answers are relatively simple. They need only introduce one new concept that is not in the question—that of a higher-order class represented by some part of the question. Such answers are fairly acceptable. The introduction of a new concept would save them from lexical inappropriateness in the core area (see p. 42); their relative simplicity, from lexical inappropriateness in the residual area. Thus we might be able to describe subjects who use categorization as subjects who avoid making lexical errors as we have defined them.

TABLE 10.48 *'When' and 'where' mode 1, related to grammatical presupposition*

	Girls				
	Q.1, mode 1	*Q.18, mode 1a*	*Q.2, mode 1*	*Q.4, mode 1+*	*Q.6, mode 1+*
Grammatical <max. presupposition	+06	−06	−10	+03	+04

The link between categorization and grammatical presupposition could have a similar explanation, a preference for brevity. An alternative view that it stems from a concern for precision and not just brevity would be consistent with the earlier results showing a strong correlation between categorization and the use of objective modes for 'when' and 'where' questions (see Table 10.36), but the third side of the relationship required to support this idea gives no support for this possibility (see Tables 10.48 and 49).

TABLE 10.49 *'When' and 'where', mode 1, related to lexical inappropriateness*

	Girls				
	Q.1, mode 1	*Q.18, mode 1a*	*Q.2, mode 1*	*Q.4, mode 1+*	*Q.6, mode 1+*
Lexical inappropriateness	−13	−13	+03	−18	−21

(b) FOCUS ON THE PROPOSITION OF THE QUESTION MODES (see Table 10.50)

Of those modes of answering for 'why' questions which we have described as having their focus on the proposition of the question, it is the authority mode which yields the greatest number of significant correlations. The girls show a pattern of relationships rather like that for the focus on empirical data modes to be discussed in the next section (iii). For boys the relationship between unspecified authority and lexical inappropriateness is negative ($r = -0.35$, $p < 0.10$).

The use of regularity and greater contextual completeness are correlated for boys ($r = +0.46$, $p < 0.01$). Perhaps for them the use of the regularity mode is simply a way of supplying extra, though not necessarily useful, information in an answer. Evidence for this is the stronger correlation between regularity qualified and total regularity than that between regularity alone and total regularity (see p. 210), just as its positive association with less than maximal grammatical presupposition ($r = +0.40$, $p < 0.05$) might also indicate a tendency to supply a greater number of information items than is strictly necessary.

TABLE 10.50 *Authority related to aspects of form and context*

	Girls									
	Grammatical inappropriateness	*Grammatical mistakes*	*Lexical inappropriateness*	*Contextual inappropriateness*	*Grammatical incompleteness*	*Lexical incompleteness*	*Vague lexis*	*Contextual incompleteness*	*Grammatical < max. presupposition*	*Lexical presupposition*
M. authority: Specified	00	00	+08	−02	−18	+17	++ +34	−19	++ +28	+19
Unspecified	−11	+05	+ +23	−18	+ +26	−06	+01	++ −30	+03	−09

(c) *FOCUS ON EMPIRICAL DATA MODES (see Tables 10.51, 52 and 53)*

The most obvious pattern which emerges here is one of positive relationships between what one might regard as less acceptable and less precise aspects of answering, particularly with grammatical

TABLE 10.51 *Cause and consequence related to grammatical mistakes and vague lexis*

	Girls					
	P. cause	*S. cause: Proximal*	*Distal*	*P. consequence*	*M. consequence*	*S. consequence*
Grammatical mistakes	00	−08	++ +27	+04	++ +28	++ +32
Vague lexis	+14	+08	++ +32	+13	++++ +44	+++ +37

mistakes and vague lexis, and the cause-effect modes. This is especially true for the girls. Distal cause for the girls behaves in a similar way to proximal cause for boys. We have already noted (see p. 234), that distal cause was perhaps the more 'typical' use of cause for girls, but not so for boys. Among the girls negative emotions acts like cause and effect in these relationships.

TABLE 10.52 *Proximal and distal cause related to aspects of form and context*

	Girls		Boys	
	S. cause: Proximal	*Distal*	*S. cause: Proximal*	*Distal*
Grammatical inappropriateness	+18	−03	−30	+07
Grammatical mistakes	−08	++ +27	+ +33	00
Lexical inappropriateness	−05	++ +30	+ +32	−07
Contextual inappropriateness	+02	+09	−07	+11
Grammatical incompleteness	+21	+19	+10	+07
Lexical incompleteness	−03	−05	+ +33	+03
Vague lexis	+08	++ +32	++ +43	+17
Contextual incompleteness	−14	++ −27	+24	+21
Grammatical<max. presupposition	−02	+14	−02	+04
Lexical presupposition	−17	+++ +36	+23	−11

TABLE 10.53 *Negative emotions related to aspects of form and context*

	Girls									
	Grammatical inappropriateness	Grammatical mistakes	Lexical inappropriateness	Contextual inappropriateness	Grammatical incompleteness	Lexical incompleteness	Vague lexis	Contextual incompleteness	Grammatical < max. presupposition	Lexical presupposition
M. emotions: Negative	−02	++++ +52	++ +31	−02	+09	++ +35	+++ +42	−13	−05	+03

SUMMARY AND CONCLUSIONS

For the girls, then, we can separate out a group of 'why' modes which tend to be associated with the greater contextual completeness (except in the case of physical and moral consequence) and with a relatively high incidence of inappropriateness, incompleteness, and presupposition in answering. These modes include authority, negative emotions, cause and consequence. They are particularly associated with grammatical mistakes and vague lexis.

Grammatical mistakes is a category of inappropriateness that occurs outside the core area of the answer, so that it could be described as a less essential sort of inappropriateness. Vague lexis may serve as a device for supplying a maximum of possible information where there is unwillingness or inability to supply a more precise term. In some cases it could be said to constitute an illegitimate form of lexical presupposition.

The boys suggest a somewhat similar tendency with certain cause-effect mode categories. However, physical cause and proximal social cause are deviant in being negatively related to grammatical incompleteness and grammatical inappropriateness respectively.

The explanation for the way in which these modes are related to formal and contextual features might be in terms of a willingness to subordinate considerations of precision, formal correctness and even accuracy to the task of tackling the answer in a more meaningful way by working out what are the possible empirical determinants of the thesis referred to in the question. Such an explanation may hold more for girls than for boys, among whom causal answers are more frequent (correlation with sex, total cause, $r = +0.49$, $p < 0.001$; physical cause, $r = +0.41$, $p < 0.001$). Also if we were to take the view that proximal cause were simpler and of less explanatory value empirically than distal cause, we might infer, on the basis of a correlation between sex (boys) and proximal cause ($r = +0.29$, $p < 0.01$), that, although boys were more likely to give a larger number of causal answers, these were of a less demanding kind.

We have already remarked that the association between authority and the empirical modes might be a function of the age of the sample (p. 249). A more positive association between authority and the inappropriateness, incompleteness and presupposition features of form and context does not hold for the boys, although it does for the girls.

(iv) Relationships between modes of answer for both 'non-why' and 'why' questions and features of form and context for answers to 'non-why' questions

This section attempts to summarize the evidence and ideas mentioned in the previous two sections, (2) and (3), under headings which are applicable to answers to both 'why' and 'non-why' questions and which have some degree of explanatory power.

(a) *THE PREFERENCE FOR ACCEPTABILITY*

We assume that subjects had some idea of what would constitute acceptable answers to the various questions asked them in this investigation, although they probably would not have a meta-language sufficient to describe their ideas of acceptability in any detail. We assume that at least some of the categories we have separated out are relevant to such notions of acceptability. A third assumption is that subjects will attempt to give acceptable rather than unacceptable answers. Ideas about what is acceptable may differ among the subjects, and individuals may be more or less proficient at fulfilling the necessary conditions in the various areas we have outlined. Awareness of stable objective standards of acceptability may also vary by subject.

Among the boys we find that the acceptable modes of answer for 'when' and 'where' questions are positively correlated with objectively and normatively acceptable form and content and also with the supplying of relatively large amounts of information. Thus those boys who are aware of what is required of them in an answering situation such as this tend to be able to supply relevant and adequate information without making many mistakes.

(b) THE CHOICE OF ACCEPTABILITY AT DIFFERENT LEVELS

Certain modes are likely to entail acceptability in other areas or at least are less likely to entail unacceptability. Thus the use of mode 1 for answers to 'where' and 'when' questions generally involves relatively short answers of a simple, set, and often-used form to state an address, a date, a clock time, etc. Categorization as a mode of answer for 'why' questions is also generally expressed in a fairly simple (X is Y) form. The use of mode 3, relative to own age, in answer to Q.11 may in some cases represent a decision to sacrifice the use of the more static simple mode 1 for a mode for which accurate knowledge of the content was possessed by the subjects.

The sacrifice of some formal and contextual acceptability for the sake of mode preference and information value has been mentioned with regard to the positive relationships of items of incompleteness (except contextual) and inappropriateness and cause-effect modes for answering 'why' questions and to the use of unique specification for answering Q.9. We cannot say whether a conscious decision is made to make one sort of mistake (according to our categories) rather than another sort. At this stage we can only point to what is likely to be involved in answering in one way rather than another.

(c) THE PREFERENCE FOR LONGER ANSWERS

A disposition to give a relatively long answer may be the result of either a preference for giving a greater amount of relevant information or a preference for giving a greater amount of speech.

We find that, particularly for the boys, the mode 1 and 1+ answers are positively correlated with contextual completeness, and are themselves generally shorter answers than their alternatives. For the girls the causal mode is associated with contextual completeness. These relationships could be explained in terms of higher relevant information content.

When the regularity mode is given it may be as an extra item of information which is not germane to the question, but increases the amount of speech. For boys, where this is estimated to be a more typical use of the regularity mode than for girls, regularity is associated with contextual completeness and less than maximal grammatical presupposition. An association between contextual completeness and irrelevance for boys ($r = +0.53$, $p < 0.01$) increases the evidence for the two-fold function which we suggest. The two-fold function may exist within the answers of a single subject. Moreover, the lesser relevance of some items than of others may not be recognized. We are simply pointing to separations which can be made in terms of our categories of analysis and the implications we see in them.

Chapter 11   The taxonomic scheme: summary and conclusions

1   Introduction

There are at least two different perspectives from which we can categorize answering behaviour, and these may diverge greatly when the answerers are young children. On the one hand, we can try to make our categories as systematic and meaningful as possible in terms of the formal, contextual and semantic characteristics of the data. On the other hand, we can emphasize the essential differences of approach to answering from the point of view of the answerer. We have tried to do both, although the integration between the two approaches may not be as complete as we should like. We know too little about children's thinking in relation to answering questions to be able to classify their responses using psychological terminology, and even if we did use such a classification we should eventually want to know how the psychological differences corresponded to the different formal, contextual and semantic features of their verbal behaviour.

Our categories represent linguistic and logical distinctions which were chosen because it was thought that they might correspond in some way to important and relatively stable differences between children. The question which we asked in Chapter 9, when we embarked on the investigation and interpretation of this matrix of dependent variables, was whether the categories of analysis gave stable patterns of co-occurrence and dissociation by user, such as: (1) to suggest they represent real alternatives rather than arbitrary divisions, and (2) to allow us to make higher-order statements about them. In this chapter we attempt to summarize the findings relevant to this question. We shall also discuss the implications of these findings and suggest how the scheme might require modifications in future applications.

We can say that the analysis reported in Chapter 10 has led us to draw some conclusions as to whether the different scoring categories do express different dispositions among the subjects which are not simply a function of their social class, I.Q. or Control and Communication index. For example, we have discovered that those children who used mode 1 for one of the 'when' questions were more likely to use mode 1 for the other 'when' question for which it was scored. Secondly, we are in a position to say something about how appropriate it is to label certain of the variables in the way that we have done (if we take a label to have connotative as well as denotative significance). For example, we find that 'categorization' as we have applied it to answers to moral questions seems to represent something similar to 'categorization' as we have applied it to physical questions, even though the content of answers is often very different. Thirdly, we have sought to discover whether our scoring categories are as homogeneous as they should be. For example, we find that the subcategory 'object categorization' of moral categorization seems to have a disturbingly large number of relationships which are significantly different from those of the other subcategories of categorization. Finally, we can indicate which variables might be grouped together into more inclusive categories. Such a higher-order grouping is recommended only in a case where both the following conditions hold: (a) subjects who use one scoring category also tend to use the other or others of the proposed group, and (b) we are able to find some plausible hypothesis to account for the grouping. For example, although there may be good formal grounds for grouping together certain modes of answer for 'why' questions on the basis of their focus on the proposition of the question, our evidence that the component modes do represent some common answering disposition within the subjects is at best only suggestive. To illustrate the converse case, we can cite the finding that (again among modes of answer for 'why' questions) unspecified authority has positive relationships with cause and consequence modes. We strongly suspect that although unspecified authority can introduce empirical information, the answer is more likely to be a logical than an empirical statement when it is used in answer to moral questions. Positive relationships with cause and consequence modes may be explained with reference to the way in which the causes and consequences were learned, but we hesitate to group the three together to form a higher-order category with a common semantic label.

We can comment only on those variables which were included in the matrix, we cannot say anything about others that might have been included. We can only suggest that a mode is not homogeneous if we see that certain of its known components (i.e. subcategories) are not harmonious with each other or if the results obtained when the mode is applied to answers of one content type do not correspond to those obtained when it is applied to answers of a different content type.

In our evaluation of the scoring categories, we have concentrated on the similarity of relationships among the categories included under a common heading (e.g. subcategories of a mode) rather than on the differences between more inclusive categories (e.g. modes). We have ascertained whether we can regard our more inclusive categories as containing unlike elements, but often we have not investigated whether each of them has greater cohesiveness within itself than with other scoring categories at the same level. An exception to this procedure applies to the evaluation of modes for 'when' questions, where we have taken into account the relationship between the use of mode 1 for each of two questions and the use of mode other than 1 for the other question as well as relating together the use of mode 1 for the two questions. It was thought that such an analysis would not be very useful in an evaluation of the modes of answer for 'why' questions, where several different modes were often used for each answer and where answers were grouped and scored according to content type rather than individual question, thereby making it impossible to estimate *how* the different modes were used, i.e. as different components of one answer or as different answers. When we sought correlational evidence for the validity of the dichotomy of focus, however, it was necessary to know how the modes representing each focus related to those of the other focus, as well as how cohesive each focus group was.

Although most attention is paid to the analyses reported in Chapter 10, we have other criteria of the usefulness of distinctions made. Where social class or other behaviourally based differences between subjects are associated with a differential usage of particular modes, subcategories, or formal and contextual features of answers, we consider that the distinctions are worth preserving.

The summary is in two parts. The first consists of the evidence which is relevant to an evaluation of the scheme of analysis; the second is concerned with the construction of higher order categories. In a final section we discuss the further application of a modified scheme based upon this one.

2 Evaluation of the scheme

The summary of findings relevant to the evaluation of the coding scheme for answers will mention only that information which is interesting, either because it indicates that the scheme should be changed in some way or because it illustrates a particularly valuable separation that has been made. We shall refer to those correlations of mode with mode both within and across the 'why'—'non-why' groupings, to those of feature with feature, and to those of mode with feature, in so far as any of these seem relevant to such a summary evaluation.

We shall discuss the scheme for the analysis of answer content by modes for answers both to 'non-why' and to 'why' questions and then the analysis of formal and contextual features of answers to non-why questions.

(i) The evaluation of mode separations

(a) *MODES OF ANSWER FOR 'NON-WHY' QUESTIONS*

Those divisions of content according to mode which were used for scoring answers to 'when' and 'where' questions have shown that they do correspond to separate answering dispositions among subjects. Supportive evidence for this has been obtained, both among themselves and in their similar relationships to modes of answer for 'why' questions. The unique-person specification mode applied to the answers to one 'who' question proved to be a sensible category to score in that it possessed relationships with other variables, but the significance of this is unknown. The functional definition mode could not be evaluated, since other types of definition occurred only very rarely.

The ways in which the modes used for 'when', 'where' and 'who' questions provided a number of significant differences between behaviourally defined groups is further evidence for the validity of the separations made (see Tables 7. 3 and 7. 5(i) and 7. 5(ii)).

(b) *MODES OF ANSWER FOR 'WHY' QUESTIONS*

Three modes of answer (categorization, cause and consequence) were examined to see whether they showed consistent relationships across different content type. This was found to be so, both in terms of direct correlations within mode across content and in terms of a similarity of relationships with other variables.

The evaluation of the system of modes via an examination of subcategory relationships proved to be workable except in the case of the mode emotions. The positive and negative subcategories of the emotions mode were found to differ from one another, but a more informative analysis would require finer specificity in the scoring of whose emotions were relevant to what objects or events.

Two suggestions for changes in the modes system resulted from the examination of subcategory relationships. These involve the subcategories of regularity and the object categorization subcategory of categorization.

Regularity, when used alone, was more likely to be given by subjects who avoided other modes of answering. In these cases the subjects appear to see the regularity as a reason for the event occurring. This seems different from the behaviour of subjects who mention, in passing, at what time an event occurs in the course of some explanation involving causes or consequences. As an adjustment to the scheme we might classify the regularity qualified items together with certain other items in an *additional information* category. Such a category would collect those items of information which, very strictly speaking, are not sought by the question, but do not seem to be intended by themselves to constitute reasons and are, conventionally, often given along with reasons. Further support for the distinction comes from the correlations between the use of these categories and social class, where for girls regularity alone is used more by the working class, and is weakly associated with low intelligence test scores and low C.C.I., while regularity qualified shows weak tendencies in the opposite direction on all three variables (see Tables 7.5(i) and (ii)).

Although for girls the use of object categorization is not negatively associated with that of other subcategories of categorization, for boys there is an unmistakable negative relationship. It is probably worth mentioning here what may have been noticed during the description of the analysis in Chapter 10, that there appears to be a greater separation between the modes for the boys than for the girls. This indicates that the boys of the sample have more stable and more exclusive preferences for answering in one mode rather than another. In the light of this impression that the girls are more variable in their use of modes, we would probably be wrong to preserve the analysis scheme in its present form simply because we failed to find that this category did not stand out from other subcategories of categorization in the girls' answers. As we mentioned earlier (see p. 208), we did not think it appropriate in this context to demand that there be a more negative pattern of relationships between than within modes. All we have sought to establish is the relative homogeneity of modes, and we have not undertaken in this study to question the validity of the more basic logical separations. Given these conditions, the fact that object categorization has some positive relationships with other categorization sub-categories does not prevent us from separating it from these. Given the present evidence with boys, it does seem that the most reasonable solution is to remove what we at present call 'object categorization' from the categorization mode and regard it as an independent mode with a label like 'Appeal to property rights or value'. The positive relationships between this scoring category and the cause and consequence modes which the boys show may be explained by their using similar processes to arrive at these different ways of answering. Such a similarity of process is not a logical necessity, however, and the same relationships may not obtain for other samples with different characteristics. The correlational analysis in Chapter 7 unfortunately throws no clarifying light on this problem.

The analysis has demonstrated the value of making separations of subcategories within modes for their own sakes rather than as part of a mode validation. Both the authority mode for moral questions and the causal mode for social questions showed up differences in emphasis according to subcategory which additionally made good sense in terms of a suggested basis for higher-order categorization. The way in which self-oriented reference to negative consequences was found to be associated with categorization, authority and restatement for the girls constitutes supportive evidence about the sorts of statements which may tend to occur together in the repertoire of socializing agents. Although we do not necessarily expect modes to be more consistent within themselves than with others, evidence for the discreteness of the categorization mode is obtained from the strong positive relationships with mode 1 for 'when' and 'where' questions that both moral and physical categorization have. This does separate them from the other modes of answer for 'why' questions. The particular and shared pattern of relationships with formal features also separates physical and moral categorization from other modes and emphasizes the internal consistency of the categorization mode.

The other relationships between modes of answer for 'why' and 'non-why' questions do not suggest discrepancies in the mode system for 'why' questions, nor do those between modes of answer for 'why' questions and formal and contextual features of answers to 'non-why' questions.

(ii) The evaluation of the categories for the analysis of formal and contextual features

The analysis of the formal and contextual features of answers was based in the main upon the scheme described in Chapters 2 and 3. The major difference was the neglect of divisions of answer area into core, concordant and residual, a distinction only made after the data processing had been completed. The evaluation of the scheme rests upon two main considerations. Firstly, we need to know whether the separations made are tenable. If the observed correlations between scoring categories are very high, and hence the scores appear to be measuring a single variable, it is misleading to keep the separation. Secondly, we need to know whether the labels attached to categories are suitable; it may be that the connotative value of a heading could be enhanced by choosing a different title.

An unequivocal empirical vindication of the theoretical scheme would require a particular pattern of high and zero correlations among the scores. For example, if the level of 'grammar' functions as a unity grammatical appropriateness, completeness and presupposition should have high correlations with each other, and if 'appropriateness' is a unitary feature grammatical, lexical, and contextual appropriateness should have high inter-correlations. On the other hand, the correlations of grammatical completeness with lexical and contextual appropriateness and of grammatical presupposition with lexical and contextual appropriateness should be zero. Such a pattern would endorse the selection of both 'grammar' and 'appropriateness' as general features.

The particular scoring precluded such a simple evaluation in that lexical presupposition could only have occurred where there was less than maximal grammatical presupposition, while in a similar manner lexical substitution was only rated when it occurred in structures which were not themselves grammatical substitutions.

Not surprisingly, the observed pattern of correlations gave no such clear-cut separations (see Table 11.1). There was a certain degree of cohesiveness on the basis of the theoretical separations—more so within levels than aspects. For the girls, lexical inappropriateness, incompleteness, presupposition and vague lexis form a coherent 'lexical' group, but much less so for the boys. To an attenuated degree a similar grouping emerges with 'grammar', but the single correlations relating aspects of context are insignificant. We may conclude that there is some evidence of a correspondence between levels of linguistic analysis and the observed behavioural variation in the children.

The relationships within aspects, are not impressive, although the inappropriateness categories do have a common pattern of negative relationships with the use of objective modes of answering 'when' and 'where' questions.

Grammatical incompleteness shows little similarity to other incompleteness categories, particularly lexical incompleteness. Incidences of the incompleteness which we call 'grammatical' consist of missing elements of required structures. Lexical incompleteness is a lack of precision; it may be scored because an expression like 'sort of thing' is added to an utterance. Hence while grammatical incompleteness means that an expression is always shorter than its

TABLE 11.1 Correlations among formal and contextual features for boys and girls

Variables	1	2	3	4	5	6	7	8	9	10	11	12
						Boys, $n = 33$						
Grammar:												
1 Inappropriateness	×	08	13	35	−42	−16	−06	−05	−23	−02	−10	17
2 Incompleteness	07	×	45	−01	−05	49	−10	−10	−06	28	−04	25
3 Presupposition	−02	25	×	−07	04	14	−15	66	24	10	−05	32
4 Mistakes	17	37	12	×	−31	00	22	01	−14	53	06	06
5 Substitution	−03	24	21	20	×	−19	22	01	00	−14	00	00
Lexis:												
6 Inappropriateness	−10	14	−03	45	15	×	−01	−03	34	12	10	05
7 Incompleteness	−02	−15	13	45	12	44	×	−15	−18	10	−17	−09
8 Presupposition	−27	−23	64	15	−23	05	23	×	25	15	−35	−35
9 Substitution	−03	18	−35	09	17	26	−07	24	×	05	−13	−13
10 Vague lexis	−07	00	−21	40	−20	40	42	−24	−07	×	−10	−10
					Girls, $n = 56$							
Context:												
11 Inappropriateness	02	−07	19	−23	−05	−06	−03	07	−35	−04	×	27
12 Incompleteness	15	−24	−17	−09	−06	−09	−01	−16	−25	−20	14	×

H

complete counterpart, lexical incompleteness is likely to make the expression longer. Contextual incompleteness, a relative scarcity of information units, will probably make for a shorter utterance, but for the answers which are the data for this investigation there was no required amount of information beyond that something true should be said. For grammatical incompleteness, however, one isolates structures and can specify for each one whether or not it is complete according to rules of grammar.

There may be grounds for asserting that what we call 'grammatical incompleteness' would be better considered as part of grammatical inappropriateness. Its positive relationship with inappropriateness categories would be supportive evidence. However, we should take into account the possibility that grammatical incompleteness in the core area might differ from that occurring elsewhere. The way in which grammatical features in the core area were scored could lead to a confusion between inappropriateness and incompleteness. The only difference between inappropriateness and incompleteness in the core area is that, for incompleteness to be scored, another element could be inserted into the core item which would change the grammatical class of that item. For example, if a nominal group were given in an answer which could be appropriately answered by an adverbial group consisting of a preposition followed by a rankshifted nominal group just like the one which is given, incompleteness rather than inappropriateness is scored because the insertion of the preposition changes the group into the appropriate class. However, the subject who gave the answer may not have been thinking in adverbial group terms at all. Thus deficiencies which are included under grammatical incompleteness are possibly incidences of grammatical inappropriateness. The failure to break grammatical incompleteness on the basis of answer area leaves us ignorant of how much of its association with inappropriateness is attributable to such incidences in the core area.

There are no other obvious indications that this scheme should be modified in any specifiable ways, either in terms of the original formulation described in Chapter 2, or in terms of the particular application which gave the set of variables for the correlation matrix. We have already touched upon one likely reason why contextual incompleteness should be negatively related to vague lexis and grammatical mistakes (see p. 264). It seems advisable to control in some way for the amount of speech given.

Certain individual categories were found to justify their independent existence. Vague lexis, particularly among the boys, was found to differ in some ways from other types of lexical incompleteness. Although the aspects at the level of lexis were positively related together for the girls, lexical inappropriateness alone of all lexical and all inappropriateness categories had a significant negative relationship with the categorization mode for both physical and moral 'why' questions as used by both boys and girls.

A kernel of categories consisting of grammatical mistakes, lexical inappropriateness and vague lexis emerges. They are related positively with one another and have positive relationships with other inappropriateness, incompleteness and presupposition categories at grammatical and lexical levels. The three kernel categories also relate in similar ways with certain of the mode variables.

3   Construction of higher-order categories

As we have suggested no higher-order groupings for formal and contextual features alone (except by implication), our discussion of the higher order categories based upon the correlational data will be separated from those which apply to modes for 'non-why', 'why' and then the two groups together, and those which apply to groups of modes with formal and contextual features, which can be subsumed under a common semantic heading.

(i) Higher-order categories for modes of answer

(a) MODES OF ANSWER FOR 'NON-WHY' QUESTIONS

Certain modes of answer for 'when' and 'where' questions were found to co-vary on a basis which we called their acceptability. Modes scored for answers to other 'non-why' questions could not be integrated into this group. We did suggest that a 'person' emphasis might explain the link between the use of the person specification mode for a 'who' question and the reference to own age mode for one 'when' question, but we have insufficient evidence to say more about this.

(b) MODES OF ANSWER FOR 'WHY' QUESTIONS

A logical separation of modes into focus on the proposition of the question and focus on empirical data categories was made. Correlational evidence gave more support for the validity of the second than for that of the first. The system of modes and subcategories was not devised with this dichotomy in mind, however, and although we did try to select out the most likely exemplars of the two foci, we were not able to put sufficient confidence in the representativeness of the selected variables, particularly those associated with a focus on the proposition of the question, to accept the correlational evidence as final. The cause and consequence modes were very strongly related together. Specified authority, which is also designated an empirical data mode, correlated positively with cause and consequence, but so did unspecified authority, although less strongly. We would therefore hesitate to make this grouping until we can disentangle how much of the relationship between authority and cause and consequence is due to the particular function of authority for thinking and learning in children of this age.

We can with confidence separate out a cause-effect category of modes which is associated with empirical relationships, and, even on the basis of the correlational data with its above-mentioned limitations, we have sufficient evidence to suggest that a dichotomous classification of modes according to their logical or empirical focus may be a behaviourally meaningful one.

(c) MODES OF ANSWER FOR 'NON-WHY' AND 'WHY' QUESTIONS

Mode 1 as it is applied to both 'when' and 'where' questions and categorization as it is applied to both physical and moral content 'why' questions were found to be positively related together particularly for the girls of the sample. The basis that was suggested to account for this grouping is compounded of the shared simplicity both of their form and of their relationship with the question, their relative acceptability and their static emphasis. They are safe modes of answer.

(ii) Higher-order categories for modes and formal and contextual features

It was suggested that the acceptability factor which was said to account for the positive relationship between certain modes of answer for 'when' and 'where' questions might also explain their association with greater appropriateness and completeness.

It seems that those modes involving greater reference to empirical data are associated with greater contextual completeness—that is higher information content. They are also associated with a greater number of grammatical mistakes and vague items of lexis. We do not know how much the amount of speech alone gives rise to a relatively high incidence of 'weaknesses' of this sort. It might be feasible to suggest that the statement of more complicated relationships would also be more likely to lead to their occurrence regardless of amount of speech. The simple, static mode categorization does not relate positively with such categories and is, moreover, negatively related to lexical inappropriateness, and we suggest that, although the formal and contextual features were not counted for modes of answers for 'why' questions, there might be a differential disposition between children as to whether they will subordinate considerations of form to those of content or vice versa. Whether such a disposition involves conscious choice or necessity due to ignorance either of content or of formal precision and accuracy we do not know.

4   Conclusions and implications

Although the taxonomy for categorizing linguistic aspects of answers to questions has not received strong vindication either from the examination of differences between groups of children or from the correlation matrix describing the co-variation of attributes of answers only a small number of features proved to be of no use. The grammatical, lexical and contextual levels of analyses can additionally be justified on linguistic grounds, and, since they also represent essential features to be learned by anyone acquiring competence in answering questions verbally, they are useful separations to make. Appropriateness and completeness can be accorded similar justification.

Presupposition at the levels of grammar and lexis did not provide interesting correlates. Of the aspects, it and substitution are distinguished by being optional features. There is neither a gain nor loss of information involved when acceptable forms of presupposition are used; only a question of a little extra effort, either to avoid it or include it. Further, although it may be conventional for educated speakers to use maximal presupposition except under special circumstances, such as in a teaching situation or where rhythmic considerations are relevant, the observance of these conventions does not appear to have normative force, and we do not use this device to identify categories of person. Only at the level of context does presupposition become significant, and here differences and relationships begin to emerge, with the working-class children manifesting more inappropriate contextual presupposition (see Chapter 6).

Because the additional aspect of answer area, with its divisions of core, concordance and residue, was not examined empirically, no evaluation of its usefulness can be made.

The modes for 'when' 'where' and 'who' proved useful in all analyses. That any analysis which involves prior expectations about the appositeness of one mode rather than another needs to take into prior account 'the associated network of relevance' was highlighted by the mode switching of middle-class children across 'when' questions. Hence attempts to make universal predictions about 'role specification' or 'names', 'absolute', 'relative to present time or place', 'relative to self' and 'relative to other time or place' will have to be tempered by sociolinguistic rules relevant to particular question-answer exchanges.

The modes of 'why', we would recommend, should be left very much as they are. Although 'Denial of oddity' 'Appeal to essence' and 'Appeal to analogy' did not occur, they might well be useful in other situations. 'Restatement of question', 'Appeal to authority', 'Appeal to emotions or wishes', 'Appeal to categorization', 'Appeal to cause' and 'Appeal to consequence' have each justified their existence. The content validity tests did suggest that a new mode, 'Appeal to property rights or value' (object categorization), be created, and its most reasonable fate must await further investigation. It was also proposed that logically superfluous but conventionally acceptable extra information given in the context of other modes should be treated as a separate 'additional information' category. How far the higher-order groupings of modes will prove successful is difficult to predict. The division between 'Focus on the proposition' and 'Focus upon empirical data' has a hopeful simplicity, and the fact that the 'Focus on the proposition' modes require only a minimal knowledge of sentence frames to generate answers to a wide range of questions may have considerable relevance to socialization practices and consequences.

The subcategories to be scored within modes are probably best considered afresh in each new situation. The types of emphasis will differ from investigation to investigation, and the empirically useful divisions will vary accordingly, although we would expect that the types of separation made are those likely to prove generally helpful and that refinements in delicacy may be sufficient for many purposes.

The separations made have been taken only to a limited level of delicacy. Finer distinctions could have been utilized, but with the particular data in hand we suspect that finer distinctions would not have been fruitful. With larger corpuses from older, longer-educated subjects further refinements would be needed. What we hope is that these changes would indeed be based on refinements rather than a redrafted scheme. Both the social differences and linguistic co-variation studies support the basic utility of the divisions made, and we therefore hope that the system will be generally useful to social scientists working in this area.

5   Applications of the taxonomy

Through Chapters 9 and 10 we have worked a painstaking analysis of a largish correlation matrix of aspects of answers gathered from a relatively small sample of seven-year-olds to a small sample of questions. We might have shortened the task by using a principle component, factor or cluster analysis, but the use of any of these techniques makes assumptions about the general structure of the relationships between variables that we did not wish to make. Better to immerse oneself in the matrix and juggle with it. Certainly the analysis has not yielded up such dramatic insights into the nature of answering behaviour that crucial experiments highlighting fundamental issues in sociolinguistic theory can be performed. Neither has it justified the taxonomy with such force and clarity that the categories used are unlikely to need amendment for other types of respondents answering different questions in other contexts.

The absence of dramatic insights is not alarming. The type of study required at any point of time is a function of the state of knowledge and understanding of the problem in hand. At the earliest phases of investigation in an area, case studies supported by speculative guesses may well be appropriate. In much more advanced phases experiments can be performed to evaluate the usefulness of tightly structured theories intended to explain the full range of relevant behaviour. At some phase it becomes desirable to have a comprehensive taxonomy of the behaviour so that empirical investigations have a framework within which to collect facts for future explanation. This is what we have attempted to do for answers to some open-ended questions.

We would hope, however, that the taxonomy should have some general applicability in the basic divisions made and the data do give grounds for some optimism in this respect. Those features of mode, context, lexis and grammar which behaved as linguistically separable units in the correlational analysis of Chapter 10 tended to be those which differentiated between the answers of the socially defined groups of children and mothers in Chapters 5, 6, 7 and 8, with the supplementary advantage that there appeared to be much common ground between the behaviourally useful and the linguistically satisfactory categories of analysis. This symbiosis gives encouragement to the notion that the categories have some empirical and conceptual viability. The evidence from the cross-checking in Chapter 10 gives a similar picture of a sufficient degree of consistency overall to heighten this.

While such results may be an artefact of the particular investigation, it could be argued that to obtain this set of meaningful relationships within such a context, paradoxically implies a wide applicability for the coding scheme. If we are able to show that the scheme of analysis works with relatively unreliable data on small samples of subjects, it should work better with more stable scores from more tightly defined and larger groups of subjects.

On the behavioural side our concern throughout has been to examine socially based differences in verbal behaviour within the framework of Bernstein's theoretical propositions about the nature and location of 'restricted' and 'elaborated' codes of language use. We have not been concerned with the absolute levels of performance of either the children or their mothers.

If, however, we accept a prescriptive view that the educational system should equip children to answer questions 'properly', then the data can be re-examined from this perspective. The very labels of 'appropriateness' and 'completeness' given to the aspects of answers are themselves in part evaluative, with the proviso that since the question-answer exchange is essentially a problem in communication a measure of incompleteness and presupposition may be desirable and some inappropriateness may not result in a breakdown of communication.

The results could be viewed in this light, and we could examine the extent to which children deviate from an 'ideal' performance. Our data give information relevant to the likely 'deficiencies' of only one particular age-group of children, but it should not be difficult for teachers to collect data appropriate to the particular children with whom they deal. The lower-working-class children, in particular, failed to give 'satisfactory' answers to some very elementary questions. This is not to assert that they could not tell a stranger where they lived, but that they did not. In so doing they were failing to use one basic function of language—transmission of relevant facts to another person and failing also to 'take the role of the other'. It is sometimes suggested that one of the reasons why lower-working-class children perform relatively badly in school is that they do not acquire sound foundations upon which to build a secondary structure. To be competent at meeting the formal and contextual requirements of answering questions might well be an essential feature of such foundations.

It is unfortunate that the classificatory scheme given here is embedded in a context of academic jargon and statistical analysis sufficiently web-like to render it relatively inaccessible to teachers. This is unfortunate, but possibly unavoidable at this stage of the game.

Hopefully at some time in the future a simpler presentation may be given so that clear, appropriate and complete answers can be offered in reply to questions about this area of inquiry.

Appendix B Coding frame for answers to 'wh' questions

Although several chapters have gone into details beyond the interest of most behavioural scientists, we have not in fact presented sufficient information for someone to score answers to questions in the same way that we have done. What follows is a detailed account of the scoring procedure, generally taking the form of a definition followed by examples, with brief comments on difficulties encountered.

The coding frame is an application of the principles outlined in Chapters 2 and 3 to the particular set of data with which we had to deal. Some categories mentioned earlier are omitted because they did not appear with any useful frequency in the data.

The categories are introduced in the following order:

> Non-why questions: Inappropriateness
> Incompleteness
> Presupposition
> Miscellaneous

> Modes of answers: Who, Where, When
> Why: Physical, moral, social
> Why: Moral

The coding frame for inappropriateness, incompleteness, presupposition, substitution and other miscellaneous non-mode categories

Introduction

THE QUESTION TYPES

The questions selected to have their answers coded on this basis are grouped into types A C D E F as follows.

Question type	Interrogative markers	Question no.	Question
A	Who	9	Who gives you lessons at school?
	Who	12	Who is the man that sees you when you are ill?
	When	1	When do you go home from school?
	When	11	When did you start at Infant School?
	When	18	When was your birthday?
	Where	2	Where is your home?
	Where	4	Where does your best friend live?
	Where	6	Where is your favourite sweet-shop?
C	What (is)	5	What is a friend?
	What (is)	10	What is a school?
D	How (to do)	7	How do you buy sweets?
	How (to do)	15	Can you tell me how to ride a bicycle?
E	How well	8	How well can you read?
	How tall	22	How tall would you like to be when you are grown up?
F	Where...from	17	Where does milk come from?
	Where...from	28	Where does the water in the tap come from?

No 'why' questions are included, for the reason given in the Revised Coding Frame for Total Answers to Moral Questions (Section 1(*d*)). Answers to Q.24 (How do the leaves fall off the trees?) were found to be too dependent on those given to the previous question, 23 (Why do the leaves fall off the trees?), to make its inclusion sensible. It was also found that the Q.3 and Q.19 making up type B (What is a home for? What are birthdays for?) were interpreted in different ways by different children and so no analysis of them was made.

THE SUBJECTS AND THE EXAMPLES

The coding frame was originally developed for the responses of the 28 seven-year-old boys whose answers form the majority of examples. It proved equally viable for their 28 female counterparts and for the 64 middle-class boys and girls who were interviewed. Examples have been taken from the answers of these later analysed sections of the sample to supplement those supplied by the 28 boys, in order to demonstrate the use of scoring categories for each question type. Some features, however, did not occur within a question type.

Where possible, relevant parts of the example answers have been marked either by italic type or omission marks to make clear the reason for their inclusion in a given category. The same answer may serve as an example of more than one scoring category, a different feature being marked on each occasion.

DIVISIONS BETWEEN AND WITHIN CATEGORIES

'Inappropriateness', 'Incompleteness', 'Presupposition' and 'Substitution' are overall headings for groups of subcategories. There is a broad division between grammatical, lexical and contextual aspects, while other subcategories may occur alongside or within these. The other categories, 'Misuse of prepositions "up" or "down"', 'Functional definition for type C', 'Information units', and 'Uninformative answers', have been applied to specific questions.

It is not always easy to decide how best to apply these categories; one answer may seem justifiably suited to inclusion in either or more than one category, e.g. Q.8, 'Good'. This answer may represent a decision to use an adjective in answer to a question demanding an adverb, thus scoring under the category 'Grammatically inappropriate answer'. It could be, though, that for a particular subject, 'good' functions as an adverb, and that it represents a 'Grammatical mistake'. It was decided that all answers containing this inappropriate part of speech would be considered 'Grammatically inappropriate answers'. Another difficult margin is that between 'Grammatical inappropriateness' and 'Lexical inappropriateness', e.g. Q.28, '. . . there's *these* lakes . . . it comes through *these* things into *this* machine'. 'These' and 'this' as demonstrative determiners are considered 'Grammatical Mistakes', better replaced by more general determiners.

On the other hand, there are the following examples: e.g. Q.6, 'Up Millses'. Although 'up' may be appropriate grammatically as an answer to a 'where' question being a preposition and, moreover, a preposition of location, it is counted 'Lexically inappropriate' since 'Millses' was contextually inaccurate, the shop not being in fact on a hill; e.g. Q.7, '*By* pennies'. Likewise, the preposition here is considered 'Lexically inappropriate'.

INAPPROPRIATENESS

Inappropriateness, 1: grammatically inappropriate answers These answers do not fulfil the grammatical requirements of the particular form of question asked. This category does not include grammatical mistakes other than those criterial to these formal requirements.

Type of question	Question	Answer content
A	6	*Marsies.*
	18	*July to September.*
C	5	*You can play with them.*[1]*
	10	*Oakwood School.*
	10	It's *big.*[1]
	10	Well *to read and do sums and that.*
	10	*Somewhere* where you learn to do things.
D	15	*Because you learn it.*
	17	*To pay.*
E	8	Not very *good.*
	8	I can only read *a little bit.*
	8	Downstairs I was on Book Two and I'm nearly on Book Three now.[2]
	22	*A man.*
F	28	. . . does*n't* come from the sea.

Inappropriateness, 2: Question-answer discord The tense, number, or person of the answer does not match that in the question.

Type of question	Question	Answer content
A	18	I think *it's* the twentieth.
C	5	*People* you like best.
D	7	You get *it* with your money.
	7	By paying for *it*[3].
	15	. . . and there's wheels on *'em* and they turn.[4]
E	No examples	
F		Come *down* through a pipe.

Inappropriateness, 3: intra-answer discord The tense, number or person does not match that given earlier in the answer for the same referent.

* The notes appear at the end of the appendix, p. 339.

Type of question	Question	Answer content
A	1	*You* go home at dinner-time and come back and then go home when it's when *we've* finished school.
	18	When it was August. I know *it's* August, but I forget what day it *was*.
C	5	So you can play with them and er you can play *any* sort*s* of games.
	5	It's a girl and er *a boy* and you um play with *her*.
	10	Where people learn*s* to write and read.
D	15	*I were* riding and *see* another boy . . .
	15	I just *get* on it and all of a sudden I *fell* over.
E	8	*I'm* in the next class . . . and that's why *we're* there because *I'm* not a very good reader.
F	28	. . . then they let go and *it* all go down.
	28	. . . sometimes there*'s these* lakes, isn't there?

Inappropriateness, 4: grammatical mistakes   These include all errors other than discord (Inappropriateness, 2, and 3) or the failure to supply that part of speech demanded by the question (Inappropriateness, 1).

Type of question	Question	Answer content
A	1	In *a bit* dark.
	6	. . . you walk down a little bit and there's *this* nice sweet-shop.
C	5	*My* mate.[5]
	10	It's a place *what* you go for the day.[6]
	10	. . . what people do things in *it*.
D	15	. . . you turn round corners and when you've turned round *this* corner . . .
	15	You um put your *leg* on (the) both pedals and you put them down.[7]
	15	. . . you pull *them* things *what*'ll stop stops the bike.

Type of question	Question	Answer content
E	8	Not *that* good.
	8	*A bit* good and *a bit* bad.
F	28	. . . there's a pipe underneath the sea where (the um this whole piece) *this* all holes in it . . .
	28	. . . sometimes there's *these* lakes . . . it comes through *these* things into *this* machine.

Inappropriateness, 5: lexical inappropriateness   Although an answer may be structurally acceptable, the lexical exponents are uninformative or wrongly applied.

Type of question	Question	Answer content
A	1	When it's '*All out*'.
	1	At *home time*.
	4	. . . over the back of *me*.
	6	*Round* Bodmin Road.
	6	*Up* Millses.
	18	*Last year*.
C	5	*A friend* who you play with.
	10	It's a big thing . . . there's these ladies and they teach you *everything*.
	10	A *school* where you like . . .
D	7	*By* pennies.
	7	You *buy* them.
	15	. . . then you put your two feet on the *wheels*.
	15	. . . put your feet like that and you *ride* it.
E	22	As tall as *you grow*.
	22	*A big girl*.
	22	*Big*.
	22	Twenty inches *long*.
F	28	*The bottom of the tap*.
	28	. . . *all* holes in it.
	28	The sky um the rain and then goes through the pipes comes through *the taps*.[8]

Inappropriateness, 6: contextual inappropriateness   This category is applied to answers or elements of answers which are judged to be untrue to fact. Inadequate specification of the criterial attributes demanded by a request for definition is not scored here, but under 'lexical incompleteness'.

Type of question	Question	Answer content
A[9]	1	After *play*.
	11	When I was *four* years old.
	11	. . . I started school *five* years ago.
	18	. . . when it was *nearly Christmas*.
C	No examples	
D	15	. . . the chain goes along to the wheel*s* and makes them go round.
E[10]	22	*Nine*
	22	*An inch*.
	22	*Ten* feet.
	22	*Twenty inches* long.
F	17	*Factory*.
	28	From the *drains*.
	28	Out of the *um barrels*.

INCOMPLETENESS

Incompleteness, 1: structurally incomplete adjuncts   This category contains only those prepositionless adjuncts of which the nominal group is not a 'proper name'[11] in a maximally presuppositive answer.[12] (—— = omission by the child).

Type of question	Question	Answer content
A	1	——Afternoons.[13]
	1	——Dinner-time.
	4	——End of Green Street.[13]
	4	. . . He's——16 Ellon Road.[12]
C	No examples	
D	7	——Money.
	7	You got to go into the shop and . . . give them the money——whatever do you want.
	15	——Pedalling the pedals.

Type of question	Question	Answer content
E		No examples
F		No examples

Incompleteness, 2: structurally incomplete nominal group A nominal group head occurs without full modification or else (very occasionally a modifier without a head. If it is a modifier missing, it is generally a determiner, e.g. 'the', but may be a submodifier, e.g. 'as'.

Type of question	Question	Answer content
A	1	——Afternoons.[13]
	11	——Longtime——
	12	——Doctor.
	18	June 24th . . . Friday.
C	5	——Cousin.
	5	What is a friend? ——Playmate.
	5	——Friend that you like.
D	15	You put——foot on one——pedal.
E	8	Not much,——little bit.
	22	——Same size as my Dad.
	22	Nine . . .
	22	——Tall as my teacher.
F	17	——Cow.
	17	——Milkman.
	28	There's a pipe underneath the sea where (um this whole piece of) this——all holes . . .
	28	——Sea.

Incompleteness, 3: other grammatical incompleteness Instances of incompleteness where the result of the omission of a part of structure is conventionally unacceptable, inconsistent in context, or ambiguous are coded here, if they are not eligible under Incompleteness, 1 or 2.

Type of question	Question	Answer content
A	4	Round Chandos——
	6	Osborne——
	6	Round the corner—— Don't know what it's called.
	6	——Across the road and up and then you turn round the corner . . .
	12	I ain't got a man—— ——got a lady . . .
C	5	——Who you go and play with.
	10	It's for children to go——to learn things.
	10	——[14] Where you go when your Mums go to work and . . .
D	7	——Get the money off o' Mum[15].
	15	. . . put one leg over the pedal, then another one on——then you start . . .
	15	. . . get on it and um it——got two pedals . . .
	15	——Down and up the whole time.
	15	Hold on——the handles.
E	8	——Read a bit . . .
	8	——Can't read.
	22	——Don't want to be very tall.
F	28	. . . this——all holes in it . . . while the water comes down there——goes right through a pipe.
	28	——Come down through the pipes.
	28	From the sea (isn't)——doesn't come from the sea.
	28	. . . and you use it then when it comes out—— the tap.

Incompleteness, 4: vague nominal group head   Only 'thing' is scored under this heading.

Type of question	Question	Answer content
A	6	. . . up that little corner *thing*.
C	10	. . . It's to teach people how to er read and write and *things* like that.
	10	It's a big *thing*. It's got railings on it.
	10	Somewhere where you learn to do *things*.
	10	For learning *things*.

Type of question	Question	Answer content
D	15	. . . you hold on to these *things*, see . . .
	15	. . . and when someone's in front you pull them *things* what ('ll stop) stops the bike.[16]
E	No examples	
F	28	. . . it comes through these *things* into this machine or *thing* and . . .

Incompleteness, 5: vague pronouns This category is scored when pronouns have unidentifiable and therefore ambiguous referents.

Type of question	Question	Answer content
A	No examples	
C	No examples	
D	7	You got to go into the shop and not go give *them* the money.
	7	G' give *them* money and um you pay them.
	15	. . . so when *it'd* got me, me Dad . . .
E	No examples	
F	28	Underneath . . . there's something that's up the top w' it's right in the middle and *they* can't get it.
	28	. . . it comes through these things into this machine or thing and *they* clean it.

Incompleteness, 6: vague substitute verbs 'To do' is often the verbal group equivalent of 'thing' in the nominal group and is scored here unless it is a case of lexical presupposition. 'To go'[17] and 'to get'[18] also qualify as vague substitute verbs occasionally.

Type of question	Question	Answer content
A	No examples	
C	5	Somebody you can play with and *do* things with.
	5	Friend what you *go out* with.
	10	. . . you get a lot of things *done* easy and quicker.
	10	. . . what people *do* things in it.
D	15	You *get* your legs and you go round with the pedals.
	15	You go on the bike and pedal the wheels.
	15	. . . and you put your foot on the other one and it *goes* [17] like that . . .
E	No examples	
F	No examples	

Incompleteness, 7: other lexical incompleteness This category contains other examples of lack of specificity or of indefiniteness not included under Incompleteness 4, 5 and 6.

Type of question	Question	Answer content
A	4	*Nineteen.*
	4	*Upstairs.*
	4	*Up there some where* not *down there, up there.* I live *down there somewhere.*
	4	*Down number 10.*
	6	Just round the corner over *the* road.[19]
C	5	It's a *child.*[20]
	5	A *person.*[20]
	10	Well to read and do sums *and that.*
D[19]	15	It's a two-wheeler and there's two little wheels on *there* and then you have to ride it *like that*[21] and then . . .
	15	Hold on the handles and put your feet *like that.*
	15	You put your feet on the pedals and you you *like* put your feet up and down.
	15	. . . you get the pedal right and lean over *sort of.*

Type of question	Question	Answer content
E	8	I'm in the next class to this one not *that* one but *that* one.
	22	About *that* tall.
F	28	. . . underneath there's something that's *up the top* and it's *right in the middle* and they can't get it . . .
	28	I think it comes from special tanks *and something*.

Incompleteness, 8: contextual completeness   For Q.15 both relevant
(*a*) objects and (*b*) actions are scored.

(*a*) *Objects:* Each part of the body or the bicycle appropriately mentioned as involved in the process of riding the bicycle is counted as an information unit. A part may be mentioned more than once but is only counted more than once if it is associated with a difference in actions. Pronouns are counted in the same way as nouns.

Answer content	Score
Put your *hands* on the *bars* and your pedals on the bars and your pedals on the bars and 'n twist *them* round.[22]	3 units
You sit on it then you put your two legs, then you put your two *feet* on the wheels and then um . . .[22]	1 unit
You put your *feet* on the *pedals* and you put your handle bars on the um *hands* on the *handlebars* and you um pedal your *feet*.	5 units
You pedal it with your *feet* and steer with your *hands*.	2 units
Yes. You. There's *pedals* and you put your *feet* on them and the' and the' up' you' every time you hold on to *these things*[22] you see and you keep going like that. And then there there's *wheels* on 'em and they turn.	4 units
You go on the bike and pedal the *wheels*.[22]	1 unit

Answer content	Score
You put one *foot* on one *one pedal* and you put a foot on the other one and it goes like that. You go f' but if you do it backwards you can't go along.	2 units
Put your *feet* over the *that long bar* then get on the *saddle* then ride it.	3 units

(b) *Actions:* Each verb which expresses some action specifically relevant to riding of a bicycle is counted as an information unit. All tokens are counted so long as they are not repetitions which fail to specify separate events.

Answer content	Score
We' you *get* on it and *start pedalling* the wheels.[23]	2 units
Ride it. I 'um I were riding and see another boy how to do it and *hold* him and then it'll start him off.	1 unit
Got two pedals and you have to ride it.	0 units
You have to put the feet you have to *put* your feet on the pedals.	1 unit
You get your feet and you *put* them on the pedals and *keep twisting* round and round.	2 units
You *have to push* the pedals and *turn* the wheels.[24]	2 units
Pedals.	1 unit

Question 28

Answer content	Score
From a *pond.*	1 unit
The bottom of the tap.	0 units
From the s' isn't doesn't come from *the sea.*[25]	1 unit
Rain.	1 unit
I think it comes from *special tanks* and something.	1 unit

Answer content	Score
Well when er you er what is it now? Co'er there's these sometimes there's *these lakes* isn't there and it it comes through 'n these er it comes through *these things* in into *this machine or thing* and *they clean it* and it goes through *these pipes* and when you turn the tap on it's all clean and fresh and you use it then when it comes out the tap.	5 units
Out of the um barrels.	0 units

PRESUPPOSITION

Presupposition, 1: grammatical presupposition[26]

(a) *Minimal presupposition* means that the answer is given in the form of a new sentence of which no part depends for completion on structures supplied in the question.

Type of question	Question	Answer content
A	4	I don't know where he lives but he lives down . . . Road.
	18	I think it's the twentieth.
C	5	He is someone that you like.
	10	It's a thing where you learn.
D	7	You go in the shop and ask for whatever you want with your money.
	15	You have to push the pedals and turn the wheels.
E	8	I'm good at everything else but I'm not very good at reading.
F	28	I know what you mean but . . . I know what it is but . . .

(b) *Intermediate presupposition* means that the answer is not a complete sentence, but has some dependence on structures in the question, although not so much as it could have, viz. the answer is of higher rank than it would be with *Maximal* presupposition.

Type of question	Question	Answer content
A	No examples	
C	No examples	
D	No examples	
E	8	Quite well.[27]
	22	Very tall.[27]
F	17	From cows.
	28	Out of them barrels.

(c) *Maximal presupposition* is where the structure supplied as answer is at the lowest rank that it is possible for it to be, given the mode of answer selected.

Type of question	Question	Answer content
A	2	Green Street, London, E. 7.
	11	When I was five.
	12	I ain't got a man, got a lady, Robinson.[28]
C	5	One of your mates.
	10	A place where you learn things.
D	7	With money.
	15	Pedalling the pedals.
E		(See 'Intermediate')
	8	Just quite.
	8	All right.
	22	About five foot.
F	17	Cows.
	28	The rain.

Presupposition, 2: lexical presupposition   This category involves the use of pronouns[29] in the answer for nouns of the question when these nouns are not supplied previously in the answer, and likewise the use of the substitute verb 'do' in the answer representing a different verb in the question.

Type of question	Question	Answer content
A	4	I don't know *her* road.[30]
	4	He lives in a place. *He* lives in a shop in er Plashett Road, I think.
C	5	Well you like *him* and he's nice to you.[31]
	5	Is *it* someone you know?[29]
	10	*It's* to learn.[29]
D	7	By paying for *them*.[3] (see p. 296).
	15	You get on *it* and pedal it and you have to steer it.[31]
E	No examples	
F	17	From cows. *It* has to be tested . . .
	28	I think *it* comes from special tanks and something.

SUBSTITUTION

Substitution, 1: grammatical substitution   The answer borrows a different grammatical form from that suggested in the question, although it is semantically equivalent. Grammatical substitution has only been counted for Type E answers, where it was particularly noticeable.

Type of question	Question	Answer content
E	8	. . . I think everybody says *I'm all right*, but I don't know myself.
	22	*A big girl.*
	22	*Like my mother.*
	22	*Same same size* as my dad.

Substitution, 2: lexical substitution   Although the grammatical form of the question is retained (apart from the interrogative transformation), the lexical items of the question are changed in the answer.

Type of question	Question	Answer content
A	No examples	
C	No examples	
D	No examples	
E	8	*All right*, anyway.[33]
	22	*High* as my Dad.
	22	*Same as you* really.
	22	*Big*.[32]
F	28	Well there's a pipe and it comes up *through* the pipe.

Misuse of prepositions 'up', 'down' and 'round'

Sometimes the prepositions 'up' and 'down' are used when there is no evidence that they refer to ascension, descension or different levels. This category has only been applied to the 'where' questions of type A (2, 4, 6).

Type of question	Question	Answer content
A	2	*Down* there
	4	*Down* my road.
	4	*Up* a balcony.
	6	*Up* Millses.[34]
	6	*Down* round the corner.

A further loose use of a preposition was thought to obtain with 'round' in such expressions as the following, and these were counted separately.

Type of question	Question	Answer content
A	4	*Round* Chandos.
	6	*Round* there.

Functional definitions for type C questions

1 Question 5 An answer is considered functional if it mentions playing or other activities in the definition rather than just liking or knowing.

> e.g. *Answer content:*
>> Your um someone you like and you *play* with 'm,
>> It's a boy and he *plays* with you.
>> It's so that you can *play* with someone.
>> Person who likes *playing* with you.
>> Someone who you *play* with a lot.

2 Question 10 To qualify as functional an answer has to mention what goes on in a school in terms of learning or teaching generally, or with regard to specific activities. This is opposed to a definition which regards a school merely as a building.

> e.g. *Answer content:*
>> Er it's to teach people how to er *read* and
>> *write* and things like that.
>> It's a thing where you *learn*.
>> Where where people go what people
>> *do things in* it.[35]
>> For you to *work* in.[35]
>> Somewhere where you *learn to do things*.

Uninformative answers

1 For Question 22 Although estimates of desirable height between five feet and seven feet (for boys) or between four feet, six inches and six feet, six inches (for girls) have all been considered exempt from inclusion under 'contextually inappropriate' it is thought that those lying outside the five foot-seven inch to six foot-four inch (for boys) or five foot to six foot (for girls) limits are suspect and are counted here. Also vague answers like 'tall as a man' are categorized uninformative while 'Tall as me Dad' is not, although the criterion is not known personally to the experimenter.

> e.g. *Answer content:*
>> About big an a man. About as big as a man.
>> About five foot.
>> Not very tall.
>> Big.
>> Er well about five foot. No, I don't know really, six foot and five?

Coding frame for modes of 'non-why' questions

Who

The answers given fell into two distinct modes: (i) role specification, (ii) identification by naming. For 'Who gives you lessons at school?' virtually all answers were in one of these.

    e.g. (i) The teacher.
       (ii) Mrs Jones.

Where

Three modes were isolated; (i) that from an objective point of view in which reference to common knowledge is made; an answer which could be traced from an A–Z reference book or a map; (ii) a specification relative to present location, usually in the form of directions how to get there from here: and (iii) an appeal to shared knowledge of a specificity more private than (i), including colloquial and slang expressions which are likely to be outside the listener's ken.

The objective references in (1) were subcategorized in terms of the fineness of the specification: (1a) precise, (1b) vague. The 'appropriateness' of any given degree of specificity will be a function of contextual features. In this investigation no child gave grid references (!) or mentioned London.

    e.g. (ia) precise: criterial features number and name of road. 27 Game Street.
       (ib) vague: criterial features absence of number and/or road name. Game Street.
       (ii) You go down the end of the road, turn left and it's the second on the right.
       (iii) Up the Flats.

When

The general frame (Chapter 3) isolates four modes: (i) objective, universal reference, (ii) relative to present time, (iii) relative to own age, and (iv) relative to another event.

    e.g. (i) In 1966.
       (ii) Two years ago.
       (iii) When I was five.
       (iv) When my sister was at the Infants.

Coding frame for answers to all types of 'why' questions

Introduction

The frame was devised which adapted the modes of answer for 'why' questions suggested in the Working Paper 'Answers to Questions', 1966, for the answers to the 'why' questions given in this investigation. The questions were grouped into three types, four moral (M), four physical (P) and two others somewhat uneasily put together under the heading 'social' (S).

The frame reached its present modified form through a consideration of responses which immediately followed the question (as opposed to later responses following probes). It was then imposed upon the subsequent (probe) responses. There were certain difficulties about this application which led to the necessity for a revised frame for answers to moral questions, thus rendering the information given here about the coding of moral answers of limited value only. A revision of coding categories for answers to the other types of question would be most desirable, but it is doubtful whether it would be economical in terms of time and effort to carry it through at present.

Although a few of the answers given as examples in the subsequent sections are invented, most of them did occur in similar form to that given here.

The questions

The numbers represent the order in which each question came in the total list.

Why P, physical
16 Why does wood float?
23 Why do the leaves fall off the trees?
25 Why does a ball come down when you throw it up in the air?
27 Why does the sea have waves?

Why M, moral
14 Why shouldn't you hit children smaller than yourself?
20 Why shouldn't anyone tell lies?
26 Why shouldn't anyone steal?
29 Why should children do what their parents tell them to?

Why S, social
13 Why are people sometimes ill?
21 Why does Daddy shave every morning?

Modes and subcategories with examples

1 Denial of oddity   The validity of the question is disputed.

> e.g. P and S (all Qs.) Why shouldn't they/he/it?
> M (all Qs.) There's no reason why they/you shouldn't.
> If the example used for types P and S were given for a type M question, it might represent a restatement of question.

2 Restatement of question as answer   This mode is subcategorized by polarity, being either a direct confirmation of the condition of the question or a negation of its opposite condition.

> (i) The same polarity.
> (ii) The opposite polarity.

e.g. (i)	P (all Qs.)	Because it/they does/do.
	M (Q.14)	Because you shouldn't.
	(Q.29)	Because they ought to.
	S (both Qs.)	Because he/they does/are.
(ii)	P (Q.16)	Because it doesn't sink.
	M (Q.14)	Because you should avoid that.
	(Q.29)	Because you shouldn't disobey.
	S (Q.13)	Because they are not well.

3 Appeal to regularity   In the case of some human behaviour, this may be an appeal to tradition rather than a statement of recurrence which is found for both the physical and social matters. For P (Q.23) a division was made between appeals to regularity which stood alone and those which made this appeal, but supplemented it with other information.

e.g. P (Q.23)	They fall off in the autumn.
(All other Qs.)	It nearly always does.
M (all Qs.)	People just don't do that usually.
S (Q.13)	Most people are ill about once a year.
(Q.21)	He always has done, since he was a man.

4 Appeal to essence   The answer given is a direct tautology, offering an explanation which is a reiteration of a criterial attribute.

e.g. P (Q.25)	Because that's how it's made.
(Q.23)	Because they are only leaves.
M (Q.29)	That's what parents are for.
S (Q.13)	Because that's what people are like.

5 *Appeal to authority*

e.g.	P (All Qs.)	Because it/they has/have to.
	M (Q.14)	Because you're not allowed to.
	(Q.29)	It's good to do.*
	S (Q.13)	They must be ill sometimes.
	(Q.21)	He is supposed to.

6 *Appeal to emotions, wishes, etc.* This mode is subcategorized according to whose wishes are seen as relevant.

> (i) Those of the subject of the question.
> (ii) Those of another person.

e.g.	(i)	P (Q.16)	Because it wants to.
		(Q.23)	The tree wants to go to sleep.
		M (All Qs.)	Because they want/don't want to.
		S (Q.13)	Because they want to rest.
		(Q.21)	Because he likes doing it.

It may seem rather absurd to expect an answer ascribing wants to inanimate subjects. They did nevertheless occur, sometimes as part of an analogy, as is the example for P (Q.23).

(ii)	P (all Qs).	Because God wants it/them to.
	M (Q.14)	Because they don't like you hitting them.
	(Q.26)	Because it upsets your parents.
	S (Q.21)	Because Mummy likes him to be clean.

7 *Explanation by analogy*

e.g.	P (Q.16)	Because it's like a boat.
	(Q.23)	The trees have a rest.
	(Q.13)	Because it's like a fight inside them.

Such answers did not occur for type M questions.

8 *Categorization* The answer either assigns an object, person, or action of the question to a larger named class, or excludes it from such. Thus answers are subdivided into:

> (i) Positive.
> (ii) Negative.

e.g.	(i)	P (Q.16)	Because it's light.
		(Q.23)	Because they are dead.
		(Q.25)	Because it's heavy.

* Answers to type M questions employing general moral terms, e.g. good, naughty, wrong, were scored under mode 8 as well as mode 5 *initially*.

M (Q.14)	Because it's being a bully. (Q.20) Because it's wrong.* (Q.29) Because it's obedient.
S (Q.21)	Because he's a man.
(ii) P (Q.16)	Because it's not heavy.
(Q.23)	Because they are not young.
M (Q.14)	Because it's not kind.
(Q.29)	Because it's disobedient if you don't.
S (Q.23)	Because they are not strong.

In the example for M (Q.29) the negative element is in the 'if you don't' clause.

9 Cause and *10. Consequence* are dealt with separately for each type of question.

It is worth noting that, although answers may take a consequence form, this does not necessarily mean that subjects see any motivating purpose behind the phenomena; they may simply be pointing to effects without considering that they are reasons, thus betraying a misunderstanding of the implication of the question. Although this is particularly obvious in the case of answers specifying effects of physical events, it can also be true when other modes are used as well, as when consequence answers are given to moral questions.

Why P, physical

9 Cause The subcategories separate the location of the cause in the following ways:

(i) Internal.	The cause is attributed to some property of the subject of the question or some activity taking place within the subject.
(ii) External.	The cause is attributed to the existence of some external agent.
(iii) External.	The relevant property or action of the external agent is mentioned.
(iv) Interactional.	The cause is attributed to the interaction of two or more factors.

Where an agent not mentioned in the question is cited it may be either (*a*) the wind or (*b*) some other agent.

e.g.   (i) (Q.16)   Because it's not so heavy.

* Answers to type M questions employing general moral terms, e.g. 'good' 'naughty', 'wrong', are scored under mode 5 as well as mode 8.

(Q.23) Because the tree does not let any water up to them.
(Q.25) Because it's got so much weight.
(Q.27) Because the other water under it pushes it up all over.

The examples for Q.16 and Q.25 seem to be moving away from the simple category answer, which they resemble, to relating a property of the object to its situation. For Q.23 the tree as well as the leaves are considered internal for the purpose of comparability with the other physical questions.

> (ii) (Q.16) Because of the current. (Q.23) Because it's cold. (Q.25) Gravity makes it. (Q.27) When it's windy it has waves.
> (iii) (Q.16) Because the water can carry it. (Q.23) When boys throw stones at the tree that knocks them off. (Q.25) Gravity pulls it down. (Q.27) Because the wind blows and wooshes it up.
> (iv) (Q.16) Because it is not so heavy as water and it can hold it up. (Q.23) The stalks get loose and can easily be blown off. (Q.25) Because it's heavier than the air. (Q.27) Because the wind pushes it down and there's no room for it to go, so it all comes up.

10 Consequence   Information is given about what follows the events of the question. These effects are of two sorts.

> (i) Man-centred
> (ii) Other

e.g. (i) (Q.16) So that we can build boats. (Q.23) Because they look all nice when the new ones come. (Q.25) So you can keep on playing with it. (Q.27) If not it would be all still and no good for paddling in.
(ii) (Q.16) So that everything doesn't get dragged to the bottom. (Q.23) So that new ones can grow. (Q.25) Otherwise things wouldn't stay on the earth. (Q.27) So there can be tides.

Why M, moral

9 Cause   The type and form of question did not allow for this mode of answer as a first response.

10 Consequence   The reason for performing or refusing to perform an action is given in terms of its effect. Orientation may be towards some positive good effect or away from some ill-effect.

(i) Approach.
(ii) Avoidance.

These two categories are each subdivided according to which of the following is considered:

(*a*) The short term effect for oneself.
(*b*) The long term effect for oneself.
(*c*) The effect short or long term, for another person.

e.g. (i*a*) (Q.29) Because they get treats and things then.
(i*b*) (Q.20) Because if you always tell the truth people will come to trust you.
(i*c*) (Q. 26) Because if people's things don't get stolen they don't have to worry.
(ii*a*) (Q.26) Because you get put in prison if you do.
(ii*b*) (Q.29) Otherwise you won't ever learn the right things to do.
(ii*c*) (Q.14) Because you might really hurt them.

Why S, social

9 Cause The scoring categories are not identical for the two questions. Causal answers to Q.13 are categorized according to the nearness of cause and then according to how general or specific it is. Those to Q.21 are first categorized as to whether they are internal or external to the subject's body and then, within these categories, relative proximity is scored. There are three sets of subcategories.

(i) Proximal. A relatively immediate cause is given.
(ii) Distal. A relatively remote cause is given.
1 Internal. The cause is attributed to some property or activity within the subject's body.
2 External. The cause is attributed to something outside the body.
(*a*) Specific. The cause is given a particular name.
(*b*) General. The cause is more one of a class which is given.

Q.13 is scored on proximal/distal and specific/general dimensions.

e.g. (i*a*) Because they catch a cold.
(i*b*) Because they get a germ.
(ii*a*) Because they go out when it's cold.
(ii*b*) Because they do silly things.

K

Q.21 is scored on internal/external and proximal/distal categories.

    e.g. 1 (i) Because he's got whiskers.
       1 (ii) Because of his glands.
       2 (i) Because Mummy makes him.
       2 (ii) Type 2. (ii) did not occur.

10 Consequence The subcategories refer either to the polarity of the central verb or the presence of the adverb 'otherwise'.

          (i) Positive
          (ii) Negative.

e.g. (i) (Q.13)	Because then they can stay away from school. (Q.21) So that he looks clean.
(ii) (Q.13)	So they don't get it again. (Q.21) Otherwise he will grow a beard.

For Q.21 only there are three further subcategories of purpose:

          (*a*) Immediate purpose only.
          (*b*) Social value.
          (*c*) Physical value.

    e.g. (*a*) To shave off hairs.
       (*b*) To look clean.
       (*c*) So that he feels nice.

Additional categories scored with examples

1 Statement of an example The example may illustrate either the situation referred to in the question or else one of the modes of answer. Two types of example are noted.

(i) Actual.	As far as one can see, the event referred to is factual.
(ii) Invented.	The story seems to be invented for the purpose of illustration.

    e.g. (i) M (Q.14) When I hit my little brother, he's allowed to hit me back but I must never hit him because he's smaller and I could hurt him very badly.
       (ii) S (Q.13) One day when it looked sunny it was really cold and my Mum and my brother thought it was warm and he went out in just his vest and caught a cold.
       (ii) P (Q.23) Some boys might be playing football near a tree and the ball keeps going up into the tree and knocking the leaves off.

(ii) M (Q.20) If you tell someone to meet this boy at the railway station when he's really at the bus station you could cause them a whole lot of trouble and he doesn't know where to go.

2 Qualification There is explicit recognition that the answer given only partially accounts for the phenomenon of the question.

e.g.   P (Q.16) Because it is light, but some wood is light and some is heavy.

        M (Q.26) Because you go in prison, but you don't always get found out.

        S (Q.13) Because they go out in the cold and rain, but you don't always get ill then.

3 Irrelevant items Information is given which seems to contribute nothing towards answering the question. This may be true of the whole of a response or of just part of it.

e.g.   P (Q.25) It's bouncy.

        M (Q.14) I'm the biggest boy in the class.

        S (Q.13) . . . they have to stay away from school.

4 Significant others This category is only used for answers to type M questions. Persons are mentioned as they affect an individual's behaviour. These are subdivided into:

(i) Police
(ii) Own parents
(iii) God
(iv) Others

e.g.   (i) (Q.26) The police'll catch you.

        (ii) (Q.29) Your mum will tell you off. (If the parents are not made explicit, but are implied, e.g. (Q.29) 'You'll get told off.' this is counted separately.)

        (iii) (Q.20) It'll disappoint God.

        (iv) (Q.14) Their Mum won't like you.

5 Unclassified The item has not yet been coded under a mode or irrelevant, because it doesn't seem to fit.

e.g.   P (Q.16) Because it's on the water.

        M (Q.29) Because if they don't *they say* it's naughty.

        S (Q.23) In autumn, the leaves *turn yellow, red and brown.*

A revised coding frame for total answers to moral 'why' questions

Section I: Introduction

(a) THE QUESTIONS

It is the answers to the four questions falling under the heading 'Why M (Moral)' that we are concerned with here.
They are:

Q.14. Why shouldn't you hit children smaller than yourself?
Q.20. Why shouldn't anyone tell lies?
Q.26. Why shouldn't anyone steal?
Q.29. Why should children do what their parents tell them to?

(b) THE TERMS USED

Some of the terms used in this frame have specified meanings. When one of these more specific senses is intended, the word will be introduced by a capital letter. Which these are is indicated below:

Question: (i) The initial formulation of one of the four in (*a*) above.
(ii) A total questioning complex, i.e. the Question (i) + Relevant Probes.
(iii) A general sense of question, meaning any interrogative expression.

Types (i) and (ii) will be introduced by capital letters; type (iii) will not.

Answer: (i) A total Answer to the total questioning complex (Question (ii)).
(ii) A general sense of answer (parallel to question (iii)).

Type (i) will be introduced by a capital letter; type (ii) will not.

Response

(i) a total block of speech immediately following a Question (i) or a Probe, terminated either by an experimenter's Probe or by some terminating sequence of the subject.
(ii) any discrete codable section of Response (i).

Types (i) and (ii) will both be introduced by capital letters.

Probe

Probe is used in only one sense here. It is a question (iii) which follows a subject's Response (i) and of which the content is in part determined by that Response. It functions to elicit, more information subsequent to the first Response (i). A Probe may consist of a repetition of the Question (i).

All instances will be introduced by capital letters.

The meaning of other terms used should become clear as they are introduced.

(c) *THE SUBJECTS AND THE EXAMPLES*

Where instances of coded categories occurred in the speech, examples from each of the four Questions are given to illustrate each.

Mode or each subcategory of Mode (see (*d*) below). These examples may come from any subject of the seven-year-old boys and girls whose Answers were analysed. With each example it will be indicated which of the three Responses is represented. They will be labelled R1, R2, R3.

(d) *THE PRIMARY INTEREST*

In classifying the Answers to these Questions we have chosen to focus upon Mode of Answers (see Chapters 2 and 3) rather than on the strictly linguistic features which were extensively examined for 'non-why' question types A, C, D, E, F. One reason for neglecting a lexical and grammatical analysis is the sheer bulk of these Answers and the long time it would require to effect such an analysis. Moreover, there is variation in the complexity of the ideas that subjects appear to be trying to express or even see as relevant, and hence they have differential opportunities for making grammatical mistakes or employing certain structures. (This may not be a valid argument, since the attempt to express a complex idea may be largely determined by the possession of structures and vocabulary necessary to make an attempt.)

We are interested in what features a subject will select as relevant when confronted with a simple moral question of this sort; whether, for instance, he looks for further ethical terms to describe the action or whether he rather presents empirical information relating to its inevitable, probable or possible effects. To what is he oriented when he is given such information or applies an ethical term—towards the *actor* of the question, the *action* itself or some *other* person? Does a posited effect lean towards the more general or the more specific end of a continuum? These are some of the relevant considerations.

(e) HOW THE PRESENT FRAME DIFFERS FROM THE PREVIOUS ONE FOR FIRST RESPONSES

The differences between this frame and the previous one fall under two main headings:

(i) Those more closely linked with the classification of total Answers rather than of first Responses for which the previous one was constructed.

(ii) Other refinements, definitions and breakdowns which were generally thought to be better suited to describing these Answers. These two are not in practice always separable, the refinements within Modes frequently being made in order to cope with those second and third Responses which seemed not to fit into the previous frame. Instances of type (i) differences are those related to decisions on Probes and Responses to Probes, links between separate Responses and repetition of earlier Responses.

Instances of type (ii) are the elimination of Mode 9 (Cause), the invention of new Modes for Responses which did not fit elsewhere, the introduction of the broad themes, Orientation and Generality, some closer specifications of the directness of the relationship of a Response to the Question, the more explicit separation of elements of information, together with further classification of type of information within a Mode or Subcategory of Mode. The ways in which its function has changed from that of the previous frame will be expounded as each mode is introduced in Section III, below.

(f) THE PROBLEMS

Decisions relating to the analysis of Answers to these Questions were found to fall in six areas which will be dealt with in more detail in following sections. They are: (a) Mode of Response, (b) Subcategory within Mode, (c) the individual element in Questions, (d) Information, (e) Inappropriateness, and (f) Probing.

Section II: The problems

(a) MODE OF RESPONSE

The Modes used are similar to those described in Chapter 3 for the classification of answers to 'why' questions in general. We have intended these to refer at some general level to how a question is tackled, what *type* of information is considered relevant and what, at this basic level, is the point of view expressed. The Modes are headed:

1 Denial of Oddity.
2 Restatement.
3 Appeal to Regularity.
4 Appeal to Essence.
5 Appeal to Authority.
6 Appeal to Emotions and Wishes.
7 Appeal to Analogy.
8 Appeal to Categorization.
9 Cause. This is not regarded as relevant in this present frame.
10 Consequence.
11 Appeal to positive Alternative.
12 Appeal to Inequality.

(b) *SUBCATEGORY OF MODE*

It is the subcategories of Modes which separate Actor- from Other-orientation, General from Specific effect, and Action from Person emphasis, as well as making various other divisions within Modes and within other subcategories of Modes. The breaking down of some Modes into various subcategories has been found necessary, both to do justice to differences in Responses falling within the same Mode and to link up common features existing in different Modes and even in different subcategories serving separate parameters.

Both Mode and subcategory of Mode will be elaborated upon in Section III.

(c) *INDIVIDUAL QUESTIONS*

Certain Questions evoked Responses which require the invention of new Modes or subcategories not relevant to the other Questions. Q.26 was sometimes answered by an appeal to property rights or value, and a section representing these was introduced as a sub-category of Mode 8 (Appeal to Categorization). Q.14 has a Mode (12) which deals with inequality of consequence. Along with the applicability of categories to only one Question goes the general inapplicability of a category to one Question. An example of this is the new 'Positive Alternative' Mode, which is only likely to apply to questions in the negative. It would seem not to carry the same meaning if labelled 'Alternative in the Opposite Polarity'.

These examples simply emphasize the fact that the four Questions cannot be said to be equivalent in terms of the Responses expected, and that each may contain for some subjects at least a 'predisposer' towards some Modes or subcategories and away from others. It might be interesting to investigate how subjects differ as to how far they examine the different Questions in terms of their individual elements and how far they will give basically the same Answer for each, representing them primarily as examples of a type, i.e. Moral. But the tendency to answer one way or the other would be limited and concealed by Mode preference. In the closer exposition of Modes and subcategories it will be made clear how far these do or do not apply to the individual Questions.

(d) INFORMATION

The amount of information contained within an Answer may be dealt with in various ways. A given Response may supply more than one Mode. It is a simple matter to tabulate within each Mode represented and to mark each separate tabulation with an addition sign to show that it is part of a longer Response. Sometimes more than one element of information is contained within a Mode or within a subcategory of Mode. It would be possible to disregard this multiple occurrence and simply show that the Mode or subcategory was represented at least once in the Response. It was thought, however, that it might be useful to note all information elements, particularly since these often carry over into a subsequent Response, and hence to classify them as to whether they constitute links in a chain of explanation or else additional or alternative elements.

Of marginal information value is the 'intensification' of an earlier Response by the addition of an adverb or by supplementing the preceding Question or Probe with a phrase containing an emphasis biasing it towards one of the Modes or subcategories. Another instance of limited information occurs when a response is a 'Synonymous expression' of some earlier response. The so-called synonymity is here defined partly by membership in a common Mode or subcategory. (When the 'synonymous expression' is of the Question or part of the Question, it is still labelled as such, but is coded as a Restatement (Mode 2).) Conversely is the case where the same salient word in a previous Response is repeated, but this is done within what we have at present chosen to treat as a different Mode or subcategory of Mode. Some of the above categories of information look like repetitions of various kinds, and with this coding they can be isolated and shifted if necessary.

Negative information is most obviously detected in the 'refusal (N.A./D.K.) Responses'. The label D.K. ('Don't Know') is applied to all total Responses consisting of some linguistic expression of refusal.

This may be 'No' or 'I can't remember', etc., rather than 'I don't know'. 'No Answer' (N.A.) is differentiated from D.K. simply by its containing no linguistically meaningful comment, although such vocalizations as 'u-u-um', 'er' may be uttered as a Response. Occasionally Responses can only be said to be 'irrelevant' because they cite some example which does not contain any elements that could be coded as informative Responses to the Question asked.

One method of presenting information is by means of examples of various kinds. There is no classification of type and place of examples as such, but the information contained is extracted and coded.

A list of information classifiers will be given in Section IV.

(e) PROBING

This area is concerned with the elicitation of further Responses after the first answer. It is necessary to determine what 'counts' as a Probe in this investigation and also, partly contingent upon this, what 'counts' as a Response.

Broadly, appropriate Probes are of two sorts, those which predispose towards the explaining of or enlarging upon a previous Response in a certain direction, and those which return to the Question, either repeating it or asking for an alternative Response to the one already given.

It has been decided to omit from analysis all refusal responses (i.e. D.K. or N.A.—see section (d), Information) occurring before the first non-refusal Response. This first non-refusal Response is then considered the first Response, and the next two Responses (if there are that many) whatever they are (i.e. refusal or non-refusal) are considered as second and third. This is providing that they follow an appropriate Probe. Even though a non-refusal Response may follow a D.K. or N.A. as fourth or fifth Response, this is *not* counted in place of the refusal.

The Probes have been roughly classified and found to have a common distribution among all categories of subjects. One classification divides Probes into 'appropriate' versus 'inappropriate', and all Responses following inappropriate Probes have been excluded from analysis here. This is maintained even when there is no fourth or fifth Response to replace them. Unlike the case of refusals following the (stipulated) first Response, we try to find a replacement for these Responses to misprobes (misprobed, that is, according to the criteria for *this* investigation), not a replacement in terms of order, but merely the elimination of the 'contaminated' Response and the consequent renumbering of subsequent Responses.

(f) INAPPROPRIATENESS

Inappropriateness related to probing is referred to in the above section (e). This section is concerned with Inappropriateness of Response.

It is not clear how far one can apply a criterion of Appropriateness to a Response to Moral Questions, since value judgments are often said to lack empirical validation. Hence the different Modes are not judged Appropriate or Inappropriate, although they may well come to be grouped on some other basis.

A Response conveying irrelevant information could be judged inappropriate in terms of its relation to the Question asked. A mis-understanding of a question expressed in Response, an 'odd' inter-pretation of it or a linguistic confusion, all might be considered Inappropriate. Linguistic confusion through which it seems possible to discern the intent, e.g. polarity 'mistakes', and apparent dis-cordances, do not prevent coding according to the presumed intent, but the above relatively rare occurrences are at present generally collected together under the heading 'uncoded'.

A Response is marked Inappropriate, however, if a dubious classification is made or a bizarre reason given.

Examples of Inappropriateness are given below in Section V.

Section III: Modes and their subcategories

The treatment of Modes and their subcategories in this section is as follows: Each Mode is dealt with in turn and following its number and label:

(a) The Mode will be defined.
(b) Reference will be made to differences between its use here and that in the previous coding frame.
(c) The subcategories will be briefly introduced.
(d) Examples will be given for the Mode as a whole and for each subcategory, when necessary. Since examples are taken only from actual Responses. there are many gaps.

1 DENIAL OF ODDITY

(a) The validity of the Question or preceding Probe is disputed.
(b) No difference from the previous use, except for the extension to Probes.
(c) No subcategories.
(d) Examples: It did not occur as a Response.

2 RESTATEMENT

(*a*) No new information is supplied in a Response which is regarded as essentially a repetition (possibly grammatically transformed) of the Question, a Probe, or an earlier Response.

A Response is only regarded as a restatement if it is a type (i) Response (see Section I*b*) rather than part of a larger Response, or if the only other information given is of the kind classed as irrelevant (see Section IV).

(*b*) The Mode has been broadened to include not only the restatement of the Question as a Response or even of the Probes as subsequent Questions, but also that of a previous Response. At the same time it has been found necessary to break this Mode down into several types. Polarity, though still retained as a distinction between Restatements, has not been found empirically to be such a useful distinction as before, since through changes elsewhere in the frame some of the devices it was necessary to employ in order to make a transformation to a statement in the opposite polarity are themselves coded elsewhere, and are no longer considered Restatements.

(*c*) Instances of Restatements are still broadly subcategorized by polarity, but are further marked according to other criteria. Of what is a response a Restatement? Of the Question, a Probe or a previous Response and, if the last, which Response?

Is the Restatement in the form of a synonymous expression which is not considered sufficiently informative to be included in a different Mode (see Section IV (ii))?

Has there been a change of orientation in the Restatement? Has the Restatement taken a generalized form?

Apart from these considerations, there is a tentative notion that it might be of value to separate 'causal' from 'central' Restatements, the latter perhaps approximating to reiteration, the former to reminder.

(*d*) Examples:

    (i) Repetition of the Question. Same Polarity:

        Q.14, R.1. Because they are smaller than you.

        Q.20, R.2. Because they tell lies.

        Q.26, R.2. Because you shouldn't.

        Q.29, R.1. Because the parents have told them to do it.

    (ii) Repetition of the Question. Opposite Polarity:

        Q.20, R.1. Because it isn't true.

    (iii) Repetition of an earlier response:

    e.g. Q.14, R.3. Because it might hurt them. (R.1. Because it will hurt them.)

Q.20, R.3. Because it is. (R.1. because it is naughty.)

Q.26, R.2. Because it does not belong to them. (R.1. Because they are stealing other people's property that does not belong to them.)

Q.29, R.3. Because it's very naughty. (R.2. Because it's very naughty . . .)

(iv) Orientation Changed:

Q.14, R.1. Because you are bigger than them.

(v) Synonymous Expressions:

Q.14, R.1. Because they are littler.

(vi) Generalized Instance:

Q.14, R.2. Because you're not to hit people.

Q.20, R.2. Because they done something they shouldn't have done.

Q.26, R.3. Because somebody has stolen something.

Q.29, R.1. Because if people tell them to do something they should do it.

(vii) Causal Connection:

Q.14, R.2. Because they are smaller than you.

Q.20, R.3. For telling lies.

Q.26, R.3. Because they stoled something.

Q.29, R.1. Because the parents have told them to do it.

(viii) Central Connection:

Q.14, R.2. Because we shouldn't. (Probe: Why shouldn't we hurt them?)

3 APPEAL TO REGULARITY

(a) When applied to Answers to Type I Moral Questions, this will amount to a reference to tradition, customs or habit as a justification for action or non-action.

(b) No difference.

(c) There are no subcategories.

(d) Example:

Q.20, R.1. Because you don't.

4 APPEAL TO ESSENCE

(a) This Mode sees the reasons for action or non-action as inherent in the character or role of a participant.

(b) No difference.

(c) There are no subcategories.

(d) Examples:

> Q.29, R.1. . . . because that's what your Mummy's for, to tell you what to do.

5 APPEAL TO AUTHORITY

(a) The justification for action or non-action is located in some constraining force which may either be unspecified or specified.

(b) An attempt has been made to separate vague from specified authority. A list of verbs denoting authority (or even compulsion) has been drawn up. The compound use of this Mode has been included, but made separable. Such responses as 'It's naughty', 'You're good', etc., previously considered as examples of Modes 8 and 5, are no longer coded here. Polarity has ceased to be a distinguishing feature.

(c) The Responses are separated out as to whether they relate directly to the theme of the Question or to some accompanying explanation or previous Response. Specified Authority is separated from Unspecified. (Unspecified instances may look very much like Restatements of the Synonymous Expression type.)

Not all occurrences of the verbs listed below are thought to qualify for inclusion in this Mode, as for instance when they are in that part of a Response which is inessential to explanation.

(d) Examples:

(i) Direct Relation:

(a) Specified:

> Q.14, R.1. It is against the rules of the school.
> Q.20, R.1. They tell some Sunday schools God said not to tell lies.
> Q.26, R.1. Because it's against the law.
> Q.29, R.2. God tells you to do it as well.

(b) Unspecified:

> Q.14, R.1. Because you are not allowed to.
> Q.20, R.1. Because you mustn't tell lies.
> Q.26, R.1. Because you're not supposed to.
> Q.29, R.1. Well if they did something like kicking people and someone told them off, you really have to stop especially if a policeman tells you.

(ii) Indirect Relation:

(a) Specified:

> Q.26, R.3. Because they [the police] 'll have to get them.

(b) Unspecified:
> Q.14, R.1. Because you've got to hit someone . . . that's big.

Verbs denoting authority: supposed to, cannot, must, allowed to, got to, have to.

6 *APPEAL TO EMOTIONS, WISHES*

(a) The general emotional element of this Mode has been disregarded. Wanting or liking for action or non-action and/or their effects are given as justifications.

(b) This differs from the previous frame in that it is broken down into simple wishes and those which are related to some other Mode (which *rarely* may not be coded, however). The Actor/Other distinction is maintained.

(c) The Mode is subdivided on two bases; Orientation: Action/Other, and Relation: Direct/Indirect. Polarity is also noted, although it is not separated in the examples below.

(d) Examples:

Actor-Oriented:

(i) Direct:
> Q.26, R.3. . . . you should pay for them if you want to get something.
> Q.29, R.3. Well they should if they wanted to . . .

(ii) Indirect:
> Q.20, R.1. Because they don't want to get into trouble.
> Q.26, R.1. . . . the police'd be after them and they don't like to so they . . . shouldn't . . .
> Q.29, R.2. Because the parents get cross and they don't like getting told off.

Other-Oriented:

(i) Direct:
> Q.14, R.3. Because they want to know. (Probe: Why will they tell their Mums . . . ?)
> Q.20, R.1. Because God doesn't want you to . . .
> Q.26, R.2. . . . because they want whatever they stealed back.
> Q.29, R.3. Because your parents like you to do it.

(ii) Indirect:
> Q.14, R.2. Because they don't like you getting gangs on people.
> Q.20, R.3. . . . and so they don't want to have the teacher do things to them.
> Q.26, R.2. Because they don't want to waste all their money.
> Q.29, R.1. They want them to be good.

7 APPEAL TO ANALOGY

(*a*) The nature of the action in Question is made better (hopefully) understood by reference to a process in a different field of discourse which is seen as similar to it.
(*b*) No difference.
(*c*) There are no subcategories.
(*d*) Examples: This did not occur as a Response.

8 APPEAL TO CATEGORIZATION

(*a*) Explanation is arrived at simply by pointing out that the action or person or object of the Question is a member of a wider class of similar actions, persons or objects.
(*b*) The previous frame's division on 'polarity' is dropped. Instead, Responses are divided on orientation and the type of attribute of the orientation aspect cited. Cases previously coded under Modes 5 and 8 ('it's naughty', 'You're being good', etc.) are contained within this mode alone. To minimize confusion, this mode no longer refers to moral consequences *following* obedience or disobedience in Q.29, but only to an evaluation of the theme of the Question.
(*c*) Orientation is divided into (A) Actor, (B) Action, (C) Other, and (D) Object. These attributes which are cited may derive from: (i) the action, (ii) the person, or (iii) the object. Attributes of the action divide into four: (*a*) Substitute is scored when the action is summarized as 'a case of X' (this again may look like Restatement, synonymous expression type), (*b*) General Moral Appeals, which apply some *general* moral term to the action, (*c*) Form of Morality, which lies on a level of generality between these first two, and (*d*) General Aesthetic Appeal, which deals with the expression of (mere) distaste and its opposite. Attributes of Persons divided into (*a*) Absolute and (*b*) Relative (relative, that is, to some other person) and those of objects into (*a*) Property and (*b*) Value, which latter may be of various kinds apart from monetary.
It occasionally happens that a judgment is 'indirect' (i.e. someone else's opinion), marked IND, or 'inferred' (it means that . . .) marked INF.
(*d*) Examples:

A *Actor-Oriented*

(i) *Attributes derived from Action*

(*a*) Substitute:
Q.14, R.1. Because it's a bully.

Q.20, R.1. Because you're a fib.

Q.26, R.1. Because he's a thief.

Q.29, R.1. If not you're disobedient.

(b) General Moral Appeal:

Q.14, R.2. Because it's being naughty.

Q.20, R.1. Because they'll be naughty then.

Q.26, R.1. It's being wicked.

Q.29, R.1. It's being naughty otherwise.

(c) Form of Morality:

Q.14, R.3. It's being cruel.

Q.20, R.2. Because He knows them don't like God if they tell lies (INF).

Q.26, R.2. Because it's being cruel.

(d) General Aesthetic Appeal:

Q.26, R.1. Because it's nasty of them.

(ii) *Attributes derived from Person*

(a) Absolute:

Q.14, R.1. [Because they're little babies and] we're big.

Q.29, R.2. Because they're little.

(b) Relative:

Q.14, R.1. Because I'm older than them.

Q.29, R.1. Because they are smaller than parents.

B *Action-Oriented*

Attributes derived from Action

(a) Substitute:

Q.14, R.2. Because [they don't like] you getting gangs on people.

Q.26, R.1. Because that's robbery.

Q.29, R.3. Because you're not to disobey . . .

(b) General Moral Appeal:

Q.14, R.1. Because it's wicked.

Q.20, R.1. Because it's naughty telling lies.

Q.26, R.1. It's not right.

Q.29, R.1. Because it's good.

(c) Form of Morality:

Q.14, R.1. Because it's not fair.

Q.20, R.1. Because it's rude.

Q.26, R.2. Because it's greedy.

Q.29, R.1. Because it's kind.

(d) General Aesthetic Appeal:

Q.14, R.3. Well it's not very nice to do it.

Q.20, R.1. Because it's not very funny to tell lies.

Q.26, R.1. Because [it's naughty and] it's horrible.
Q.20, R.1. Because it's nice [and kind].

C *Other-Oriented*

(i) *Attributes derived from Action*

(*a*) Substitute: no examples.
(*b*) General Moral Appeal: no examples.
(*c*) Form of Morality
   Q.14, R.2. [People who are unkind to you] you shouldn't be unkind to them.
   Q.20, R.2. Because it is not fair for them.
   Q.26, R.1. . . . it's unfair for the other people.
   Q.29, R.2. Because they're kind to their mothers and fathers.
(*d*) General aesthetic appeal:
   Q.14, R.1. . . . and it's not very nice to them.

(ii) *Attributes derived from Person*

(*a*) Absolute:
   Q.14, R.1. Because they are only little babies [and we're big].
   Q.29, R.1. Because they're the head.
(*b*) Relative:
   Q.14, R.1. Because they're not the same age.
   Q.29, R.1. Because they're bigger than their children.

D *Object-Oriented*

(i) *Attributes derived from Object*

(*a*) Value:
   Q.26, R.2. Because other people like it [and other people want it].
   R.2. Because it might be valuable.
(*b*) Property:
   Q.26, R.2. Well you shouldn't steal things from other people when it don't belong to you.
   R.2. Because it's not your property.

9 APPEAL TO CAUSE

Answers which might have been included in this category were in fact coded elsewhere for moral Questions, e.g. appeals to essence or authority.

10 APPEAL TO CONSEQUENCE

(*a*) The effect of the action is given.

L

(b) The title of this Mode is different from the one it bore in the original frame. It is often uncertain whether a subject responding in this form considers that the effects noted have a motivational relationship to action or non-action or whether they are simply associated consequences; the grammatical form of the Response sometimes suggests that purpose is absent when consequence is referred to, hence the rejection of the label 'Purpose'.

The previous frame divided Responses on 'Approach/Avoidance', subdividing each other as to whether the effect was on the Actor (then labelled 'Self') or some Other. Effect for the Actor was then subdivided as 'Short-' or 'Long-Term'. The present frame makes 'Positive/ Negative' replace 'Approach/Avoidance' for the same reason that 'Consequence' is preferred to 'Purpose' in the title. 'General' effect has been added to Actor and Other. 'Punishment' and 'Other Ill-Effect' seemed more fundamental distinctions than 'Short-' and 'Long-Term', although 'Long-Term' is still marked. A General/Specific distinction was also thought to be relevant to Answers in this Mode.

(c) A fundamental distinction separates 'Good' from 'Ill' effects of Action into 'Positive' and 'Negative' categories. All Responses are assigned an Orientation, viz. 'Actor', 'General', (rather similar to 'Action' of Mode 8) or 'other'. All Negative Responses with Actor or Other Orientations are seen as falling closer to one or the other end of a General/Specific dimension. Negative Actor-Oriented Responses are separated on 'Punishment' or 'Other Ill-Effects'.

Within this Mode there are special considerations applying to the individual Questions. For Q.29 certain Responses previously put into Mode 8 are now coded here. When a subject indicates that an action is done in obedience to parents, and this is likely to ensure that it is 'good', it is coded here. The related case is that where refusal to obey is seen as 'bad'. There is an attempt to keep Mode 8 for Responses referring to the value of doing what one is told *per se*. 'Inferential' Responses will be coded for Orientation as in Mode 8 and marked as such. Religious reasons were given for refusing to lie more than for other Modes for which the reason is probably clear. Such Responses as 'God hears you', 'Jesus is with you all the time' are coded in the Negative, General category and marked G. or J.

(d) Examples:

1 Positive

A *Actor-Oriented:*

Q.29, R.1. Because then they'll learn.

B *General/Action-Oriented:*
Q.29, R.1. Because it must be good.

C *Other-Oriented:*

   Q.29, R.3. To help their Mum.

2 *Negative*

A *Actor-Oriented:*

   (i) Punishment:
(*a*) General:
   Q.14, R.1. You will get in trouble yourself.
   Q.20, R.1. Because you get into trouble.
(*b*) Specific:
   Q.14, R.2. Because their mother . . . writes to the police.
   Q.26, R.1. Because if a policeman sees you he will take you away.
   Q.29, R.2. Or else you will get a smack.

   (ii) Other Ill-Effect:
(*a*) General:
   Q.14, R.2. Because you may get hurt.
   Q.20, R.3. . . . they wouldn't believe you.
   Q.29, R.1. Because they'll do things wrong.
(*b*) Specific:
   Q.14, R.1. If they hit, they got to hit you back.
   Q.20, R.2. Because people won't like you when you grow up.
   Q.26, R.2. Because they call you a liar because when you say you never did it and then you're telling a lie.

B *General/Action-Oriented:*

   Q.14, R.1. Because you will have a fight.
   Q.20, R.2. Because God is with you every time.
   Q.29, R.2. . . . when . . . married . . . won't do nice things.

C *Other-Oriented:*

(*a*) General:
   Q.14, R.2. Because it hurts.
   Q.20, R.3. Because people think they are not telling lies.
   Q.26, R.3. . . . if you steal you will waste all their money.
(*b*) Specific:
   Q.14, R.3. Because they are a bit scared.
   Q.26, R.3. If you steal too much things off other little ones they might not have anything left . . .
   Q.29, R.3. . . . they put Mummy and Daddy in gaol.

The following Modes, if they can be called such, had not previously occurred in the data formulation:

L*

11 APPEAL TO POSITIVE ALTERNATIVE

(a) Applied to Moral Questions of the present type which are in the negative form (hence excluding Q.29), this Mode collects those Responses which suggest the existence of an alternative line of action to that of the Question, either advocating it or stating that this is not an example of it.

(b) It did not occur in the previous frame.

(c) There are no subcategories.

(d) Examples:

> Q.14, R.1. Because you should pick on someone your own size.
>
> Q.20, R.3. ... you should own up to the person and tell them.
>
> Q.26, R.2. Because you've got to buy them in the shop for money.

12 APPEAL TO INEQUALITY

(a) This Mode focuses upon Responses which are concerned with the inequality of an effect (as opposed to a Response which concentrates upon the effect itself which may or may not be unequally distributed).

(b) It did not occur in the previous frame.

(c) There are no subcategories, but there may be a moral implication (marked M).

(d) Examples:

> Q.14, R.1. ... if we hit those they'll go home crying but if they hit us we don't go in crying.
>
> R.2. (for being naughty and) hitting them of nothing (M).
>
> Q.26, R.3. ... they might not have anything left and we might have it.

Section IV: information

Examples are given here of the various information types suggested in Section II.

(1) INTENSIFICATION:

This may be of two sorts:

(a) Repetition of Question, Probe, or previous Response, with the addition of an adverb.

e.g. Q.14, R.1. Because you might hit them very seriously.
  Q.20, R.3. Because it's nasty and really and truly rude. (R.1. Because it's rude).

(*b*) Repetition of Question, Probe or previous Response, with the addition of a phrase which, if given a more central emphasis, would have been coded without hesitation in a given Mode or subcategory. It is perhaps the intention that is in question.

e.g. Q.20, R.2. Because they told a lie about people.
  Q.26, R.2. Because they've been stealing from other people.

(2) *SYNONYMOUS EXPRESSION*

A Response falls within the same Mode or subcategory as an earlier Response (if as the question, it will be coded in Mode 2, Restatement). Furthermore, it seems to bear a very close relationship in terms of meaning to the earlier Response.

e.g. Q.14, R.3. Well you're doing a sin really. (R.2. Because it's not right to hit babies because it's being naughty really.)
  Q.20, R.2. Because it's naughty. (R.1. Because it's not right.)
  Q.26, R.3. Because it's a wrong thing to do. (R.1. Because it's naughty.)

(3) *RECURRENT WORD*

A Response is given in which there is a certain word which, depending upon the linguistic context, designates the Response to a given Mode. An earlier Response had contained this same criterial word, but in a different linguistic context, which caused it to be placed in a different Mode or subcategory, as these are defined at present.

e.g. Q.14, R.2. Because they are not very strong. (R.1. Because they would cry and they are not as strong as you.)
  Q.20, R.3. Because they are horrible and naughty. (R.1. Because it's naughty.)
  Q.29, R.3. It's naughty. (R.2. So they don't be naughty and they get smacked.)

(4) *ADDITIONAL ITEMS WITHIN RESPONSES:*

These may be of two sorts:
(*a*) Those more likely to fall within the same Mode or subcategory (i.e. those of Response type 2: see Section I*b*), where the link is normally 'and' or 'or' and the impression is of listing.

> e.g. Q.14, R.2. Because it hurts them and it makes them cry.
> Q.29, R.1. If . . . you might get a smack or be told off.

(b) Those more likely to fall in different Modes or subcategories (i.e. those of Response type 1: see Section Ib), where there may be a variety of links, e.g. 'because', 'so', 'and', 'or'. Here the separate parts could equally well have occurred as separate Responses with probes in between.

> e.g. Q.14, R.1. Teach them to be naughty and get told off for themselves.
> Q.20, R.2. It's better to tell the truth because if you tell lies you might get a smack.
> Q.26, R.2. Because you're robbing money from people because they might need it.
> Q.29, R.3. Because you're too naughty and have to do what your Mum says.

(5) CHAIN ITEMS:

A Response may consist of information of main and subsidiary significance. This may be true also of a total Answer, where one Response may contain such subsidiary information in relation to some other Response. The items *generally* fall within the same Mode or subcategory. It is the subsidiary items that are marked, and this may involve a degree of subjective judgment, though there are some objective criteria. When the subsidiary information is contained in a separate Response, it is in the latter Response that it is said to occur. When it is contained within the same Response, it is sometimes in the form of a conditional clause.

> e.g. Q.14, R.1. Because they'll fall over and hurt themselves.
> Q.20, R.2. They'll believe you and go and do it and get into trouble and they didn't do it . . .
> Q.26, R.3. A policeman catches him and puts him in jail.

Section V: Inappropriateness

As was mentioned in Section II, only certain types of inappropriateness are counted here—namely, 'bizarre Responses' and 'dubious classification'. Examples are rare, but are marked so that they might be extracted for an analysis controlling for appropriateness.

(a) 'Bizarre Responses':

> e.g. Q.20, R.1. Because sometimes you can get pimples on your tongue.

Q.26, R.2. Jesus tells people and they don't like them ever again.

(b) 'Dubious Classification':

e.g. Q.14, R.3. Because they are friends.
Q.20, R.3. Because you might go to prison.
Q.26, R.2. Because if someone buys things with their money well it's rude to take something else.

Notes

1 The question asks for a definition rather than an attribute.
2 Such an answer may eventually come to be regarded as appropriate as an operational demonstration of 'how well'.
3 This particular answer was ambiguous as to whether 'it' or 'them' was said, and has thus been used as an example of two categories.
4 ' 'Em' has been taken as referring to the bicycle. However, it may be intended to represent 'these things' mentioned in the previous sentence. If this were so, it would not qualify to be counted here.
5 This might be regarded as a case of grammatical incompleteness as well as inappropriateness, in which case the 'what' could be corrected to 'that' rather than 'where', and 'in' inserted after 'go'.
6 This may come to be thought lexically inappropriate.
7 If 'incompleteness' extends to morpheme rank, then this example belongs there.
8 This is a borderline judgment.
9 For Q.1 an estimate between three o'clock and five o'clock is considered appropriate, though perhaps finer limits should be drawn, especially at the earlier end (children may not go straight home).
10 For Q.22 any estimate between seven feet and five feet is considered appropriate. For the girls the limits are shifted downwards by six inches (six feet, six inches and four feet, six inches). These limits, like those of note 9, may merit changing.
11 'Proper names' are here stipulated to include addresses consisting of more than the number of house or flat, dates consisting of more than the day of the month, chronometric time, but *not* conventional time markers like 'dinner-time', 'home-time', etc. Many children answered, e.g., '16 Ellon Road' rather than 'at 16 Ellon Road'. The omission of this preposition was so common that it would be misleading to count it as 'grammatical incompleteness' or 'inappropriateness'.
12 This example is the only one where 'maximal presupposition' is relevant.
13 These answers are incomplete in two ways: as adjuncts lacking both prepositions to govern complements and determiners to modify the nominal group heads of the complements.
14 Omissions are regarded as elements at given ranks, so that if a subject is missing at clause rank, one omission is counted, regardless of how many constituent elements the particular omitted nominal group may have contained. The example contains two omissions: at clause rank the subject is missing and at group rank the verbal auxiliary is missing.
15 This girl is relating how she buys sweets. Therefore the lack of subject cannot be interpreted as a feature of the imperative mood.

16   'Thing' is still counted here, even though it is qualified with a defining relative clause.

17   'Go' is considered a substitute when a more specific verb would be more conventionally acceptable or when, as in this example, it is part of a vague phrase.

18   When 'get' is followed by 'on' 'in', etc., it is *not* counted here. Probably the same would apply if it were followed by an adjective.

19   Although such an uninformative use of the definite article is counted as lexically incomplete for type A questions, similar occurrences in other types of question have not been counted anywhere, e.g. Type D, Q.7, 'You have to give *the* lady *the* money'.

20   It was thought that such answers are too general to be acceptable as attempts at definition.

21   This might have not been incomplete, if there had been greater specificity earlier on.

22   Q.15. Whereas 1,337's answer may be slightly misleading it is indirectly accurate, but 1,118's ' . . . your pedals on the bars . . .' is not informative (although the later reference to 'pedals', viz. 'them' is) and 1,130's 'Put your two *feet* on the wheels' is inaccurate, although 'feet' do have a putting action to perform, and thus feet-putting is considered as two information units, one under (*a*) objects, the other under (*b*) actions. 1,234's ' . . . *these things* . . .' is not as informative as it might be, but have been counted as a unit.

23   'Start' is regarded as part of a compound verb.

24   The turning of the wheels is not an additional human activity, but is counted there.

25   This is counted, in spite of being negative.

26   Generally the first utterance is the criterial one for grammatical presupposition. However, maximal and intermediate presupposition may occur later in the answer, as in the example (Maximal, Q.12), where the first sentence is taken as parenthetical.

27   It is debatable whether these examples, in the face of the conventional unacceptability of their maximal presuppositive counterparts, viz. 'very', 'quite', should be coded here rather than under (*c*) *maximal*. In fact, in the final tabulations it was decided to consider such as maximal because of a putative closer relationship to other maximally presuppositive answers.

28   Generally the first utterance is the criterial one for grammatical presupposition. However, maximal and intermediate presupposition may occur later in the answer as in the example (maximal, Q.12), where the first sentence is taken as parenthetical.

29   It is sometimes ambiguous whether the pronoun refers to a noun in the question or not. In the examples, 'it' may refer to 'the answer' rather than 'a friend' or may be a 'kataphoric' reference. In a case like (Q.1) 'Think it's four o'clock' the pronoun cannot be lexically presuppositive, since there is no noun in the question that it could be substituting for.

30   This is a 'non-answer', however, and perhaps should not be counted.

31   Only the *first* instance of a given pronominal (or verbal) substitution is counted.

32   This substitution was also considered inappropriate lexically, since it is not semantically equivalent to 'tall'.

33   There is some doubt as to whether this is an adverb, but it has been counted here as one.

34   This instance has also been counted as lexically inappropriate.

35   These examples are rather weak, and tighter coding may well exclude them, but at the moment they stand as 'functional'.

Appendix C The questions asked of seven-year-old children

In so far as words in questions are stressed, those underlined should carry it.

1 When do you go home from school?
2 Where is your home?
3 What is a home for?
4 Where does your best friend live?
5 What is a friend?
6 Where is your favourite sweet-shop?
7 How do you buy sweets?
8 How well can you read?
9 Who gives you lessons at school?
10 What is a school?
11 When did you start at Infant school?
12 Who is the man who sees you when you are ill?
13 Why are people sometimes ill? (2 probes.)
14 Why shouldn't you hit children smaller than yourself? (2 probes.)
15 Can you tell me how to ride a bicycle?
16 Why does wood float? (2 probes.)
17 Where does milk come from? (If child answers 'cows', ask Why?)
18 When was your birthday?
19 What are birthdays for?
20 Why shouldn't anyone tell lies? (2 probes.)
21 Why does Daddy shave every morning? (2 probes.)
22 How tall would you like to be when you are grown up?
23 Why do the leaves fall off the trees? (2 probes.)
24 How do the leaves fall off the trees?
25 Why does a ball come down when you throw it up in the air? (2 probes.)
26 Why shouldn't anyone steal? (2 probes.)

27 Why does the sea have waves? (2 probes.)
28 Where does the water in the tap come from?
29 Why should children do what their parents tell them to? (2 probes.)
30 Tell me all the different things you can do with a piece of string.

A probe was a further question which sought an elaboration of the child's initial answer.

References

AREWA, E. O., and DUNDES, A., 'Proverbs and the Ethnography of Speaking Folklore', Gumperz, J. J., and Hymes, D. (eds), Spec. Ed., *Amer. Anthrop.*, (1964), lxvi, 70–85.

ATKINSON, J. W. (ed.), *Motives in Fantasy, Action and Society*, New York: Van Nostrand, 1957.

BECKER, W. C., 'Consequences of Different Kinds of Parental Discipline', in Hoffman, M. L., and Hoffman, L. W. (eds.), *Child Development Research*, i, New York: Russell Sage, 1964.

BERLYNE, D. E., *Conflict, Arousal and Curiosity*, New York: McGraw-Hill, 1960.

BERNSTEIN, B. B., 'Some Sociological Determinants of Perception', *Brit. J. Sociol.* (1958), ix, 159–74.

'Social Structure, Language and Learning', *Educ. Res.* (1961a), iii, 163–76.

'Social Class and Linguistic Development'; in Halsay, A. H., Floud, J. and Anderson, A. (eds), *Education, Economy and Society*, Free Press, 1961(b).

'Linguistic Codes, Hesitation Phenomena and Intelligence', *Language and Speech*, (1962a), v, 31–46.

'Social Class, Linguistic Codes and Grammatical Elements', *Language and Speech*, (1962b), v, 221–40.

and YOUNG, D., 'Social Class Differences in Conceptions of the Use of Toys', *Sociology* (1967), i, 131–40.

BRAITHWAITE, R. B., *Scientific Explanation*, Cambridge Univ. Press, 1954.

BRANDIS, W., and HENDERSON, D., *Social Class, Language and Communication*, London: Routledge, 1970.

BRONFENBRENNER, U., 'Socialization and Social Class through Time and Space', in Maccoby, E. E., Newcombe, T. M., and Hartley, E. L. (eds), *Readings in Social Psychology*, New York: Holt, 1958, 400–25.

CAZDEN, C. B., 'Subcultural Differences in Child Language', *Merrill-Palmer Qtly.* (1966), xii, 185–219.

CENTRAL ADVISORY COUNCIL FOR EDUCATION (ENGLAND), *Early Leaving*, London: H.M.S.O., 1954.

15 to 18 (Crowther), London: H.M.S.O., 1959.

Half Our Future (Newsom), London: H.M.S.O., 1963 (a).

Children and Their Primary Schools (Plowden), London: H.M.S.O., 1966.

CHOMSKY, N., *Syntactic Structures*, The Hague: Mouton, 1957.

Aspects of the Theory of Syntax, Cambridge, Mass.: M.I.T. Press, 1965.

CLAUSEN, J. A., 'Family Structure, Socialization and Personality', in Hoffman, M. L., and Hoffman, L. W. (eds) *Child Development Research*, ii, New York: Russell Sage, 1964.

COMMITTEE ON HIGHER EDUCATION, *Higher Education (Robbins)*, London: H.M.S.O., 1963 (b).

COOK, J., 'An Inquiry into Patterns of Communication and Control between Mothers and Children in Different Social Classes', Ph.D. thesis, Univ. of London, 1971.

COULTHARD, R. M., and ROBINSON, W. P., 'The Structure of the Nominal Group and Elaboratedness of Code', *Language and Speech* (1968), *xi*, 234–50.

DEUTSCH, M., *The Disadvantaged Child*, New York: Basic Books, 1967.

DIXON, R. M. W., *Linguistic Science and Logic*, The Hague: Mouton, 1963.

DOUGLAS, J. W. B., *The Home and the School*, London: MacGibbon & Kee, 1964.

DURKHEIM, E., *The Division of Labour in Society* (1st ed., 1893), trans. G. Simpson, New York: Free Press, 1949.

ELLIS, J., 'On Contextual Meaning', in Bazell, C. E., Catford, J. C., Halliday, M.A.K., and Robins, R. H. (eds), *In Memory of J. R. Firth*, London: Longmans, 1966.

ERVIN TRIPP, S. M., 'An Analysis of the Interaction of Language, Topic, and Listener', in *The Ethnology of Communication*, Gumperz, J. J., and Hymes, D. (eds), *Amer. Anthropologist* (1964), lxvi, 86–102.
'Sociolinguistics' in Berkowitz, L. (ed.), *Advances in Experimental Social Psychology* (1969), iii, New York: Academic Press.

FOWLER, H., *Curiosity and Exploratory Behaviour*, New York: Macmillan, 1963.

FLAVELL, J. H., *The Development of Role-taking and Communication Skills in Children*, New York: Wiley, 1968.

GAHAGAN, D. and G., *Talk Reform: an Exploratory Language Programme for Infant School Children*, London: Routledge, 1970.

GOLDMAN-EISLER, F., 'Hesitation and Information in Speech', in Cherry, C. (ed.), *Information Theory*, 4th London Symposium, Butterworth, 1961.

HALLIDAY, M. A. K., MCINTOSH, A., and STEVENS, P., *The Linguistic Sciences and Language Teaching*, London: Longmans, 1964.

HAWKINS, P., 'Social Class, the Nominal Group and Reference', *Language and Speech* (1969), *xii*, 125–35.

HESS, R. D., and SHIPMAN, V. C., 'Cognitive Elements in Maternal Behaviour', in Hill, J. P. (ed.), *Minnesota Symposia on Child Psychology*, i, Minneapolis: Univ. of Minnesota, 1967.

HYMES, D., 'Models of the Interaction of Language and Social Setting', *J. Soc. Iss.* (1967), xxiii, 8–28.

IRWIN, D. C., 'Infant Speech: the Effect of Family Occupational Status and of Age on Use of Sound Types', *J. Speech Hearing Disorders* (1948), xiii, 223–6.

ISAACS, N., *Appendix on Children's 'Why' Questions*, London, 1930.

JONES, D., *An Outline of English Phonetics* (8th ed.), Cambridge: Heffer, 1956.

JONES, J., 'Social Class and the Under-fives', *New Society* (1966), ccxxi, 935–6.

JOOS, M., 'The Five Clocks', *Internat. J. Amer. Linguistics*, xxviii, Part 5, 1962.

KATZ, J. J., and FODOR, J. A., 'The Structure of a Semantic Theory', *Language* (1963), xxxix, 170–210.

KOHLBERG, L., 'Stage and Sequence in Moral Development', in Goslin, D. (ed.), *Handbook of Socialization Theory and Research*, Chicago: Rand McNally, 1969.

KOHN, M. L., 'Social Class and Parent-child Relationships: an Interpretation', *Amer. J. Sociol.* (1963), lxviii, 471–80.

LABOV, W., *The Social Stratification of English in New York City*, Washington, D.C.,: Center for Applied Linguistics, 1966.

LAWTON, D., 'Social Class Differences in Language Development', *Language and Speech* (1963), vi, 120–43.
'Social Class Language Differences in Group Discussions', *Language and Speech* (1964), vii, 182–204.
Social Class, Language and Education, London: Routledge, 1968.

LOVELL, K., *An Introduction to Human Development*, London: Macmillan, 1968.

MEDAWAR, P. B., *The Art of the Soluble*, London: Methuen, 1967.

MORTON-WILLIAMS, ROMA, and FINCH, S., Schools Council Enquiry, 1, *Young School Leavers*, London: H.M.S.O., 1968.

PEI, M., *Glossary of Linguistic Terminology*, Columbia Univ. Press, 1966.

PIAGET, J., *The Language and Thought of the Child*, London: Routledge, 1926.
The Child's Conception of Physical Causality, London: Routledge, 1930.
The Moral Judgement of the Child, London: Routledge, 1932.
The Psychology of Intelligence, London: Routledge, 1950.

RACKSTRAW, S. J., and ROBINSON, W. P., 'Social and Psychological Factors associated with Variability of Answering Behaviour in Five-year-old Children', *Language and Speech* (1967), x, 88–106.

RAVEN, J. C., *The Crichton Vocabulary Scale*, London: Lewis, 1951.

ROBINSON, W. P., 'Close Procedure for the Investigation of Social-class Differences in Language Usage', *Language and Speech* (1962a), viii, 45–55.
'The Elaborated Code in Working-class Language', *Language and Speech* (1962b), viii, 243–52.
'Restricted Codes in Sociolinguistics and the Sociology of Education', in Whiteley, W. B. (ed.), *Language and Social Change*, Oxford Univ. Press, 1970(a).
Language as a Socio-cultural Determinant of Learning, Hamburg: UNESCO Institute for Education, 1970(b).
and CREED, C. D., 'Perceptual and Verbal Discriminations of "Elaborated" and "Restricted" Code Users', *Language and Speech* (1968), xi, 182–93.
and RACKSTRAW, S. J., 'Variations in Mothers' Answers to Children's Questions as a Function of Social Class, Verbal Intelligence Test Scores and Sex', *Sociology* (1967), i, 259–76.

SCHATZMAN, R., and STRAUSS, A., 'Social Class and Modes of Communication', *Amer. J. Sociol.* (1955), lx, 329–38.

SINCLAIR, J. MCH., 'Beginning the Study of Lexis', in Bazell, C. E., Catford, J. C., Halliday, M. A. K., and Robins, R. H. (eds), *In Memory of J. R. Firth*, London: Longmans, 1966.

SKINNER, B. F., *Verbal Behaviour*, New York: Appleton-Century-Crofts, 1957.

TEMPLIN, M. C., *Certain Language Skills in Children: Their Development and Interrelationships*, Minneapolis: Univ. Minnesota Press, 1957.

TURNER, G. J., and MOHAN, B. A., *A Linguistic Description and Computer Program for Children's Speech*, London: Routledge, 1970.

URE, J. N., and RODGER, A., ' "Cargoes", a Linguistic Study of a Literary Text', undated, unpublished, ms.

VERNON, P. E., *Intelligence and Cultural Environment*, London: Methuen, 1969.

VYGOTSKY, L. S., *Thought and Language*, New York: Wiley, 1962.

WECHSLER, D., *Wechsler Intelligence Scale for Children: Manual*, New York: Psychol. Corp., 1949.

WISEMAN, S., *Education and Environment*, Manchester Univ. Press, 1964.

ZIPF, G. K., *The Psycho-biology of Language*, New York: Houghton Mifflin, 1935.

Author Index

N.B. Page numbers in roman refer to Vol I and those in italic Vol II

Allport, G. W., 114
Arewa, C. O., 73
Atkinson, J. W., 8
Becker, W. C., 10
Berlyne, D. E., 8
Bernstein, B., 2, 11, 12, 35, 70–1, 72, 73, 75, 93–5, 96, 97, 98, 103, 112, 113, 115, 116, 117, 119, 121, 127, 146, 148, 150, 152–7 *passim*, *183*, *292*
Braithwaite, R. B., 66
Brandis, W., 6, 96, 99, 113, 126, 127, 150, 156
Brimer, M. A., 78, 126
Bronfenbrenner, U., 10
Cazden, C., 10
Central Advisory Council for Education, 11
Chomsky, N., 71, *vii*, *182*
Clausen, J. A., 10
Cook, J., 116–17, 127, 154, 156
Coulthard, C. M., 126
Creed, C. D., 115, 126
Deutsch, M., 10
Dixon, R. M. W., 39
Douglas, J. W. B., 11
Dundas, A., 73
Dunn, L. M., 78, 126
Ellis, J., 26, 28
Ervin-Tripp, S., 10–11, 29
Finch, S., 11
Flavell, J. H., 35
Fodor, J. A., 21
Fowler, H., 8
Gahagan, D. H. and G., 7, 121, 126
Goldman-Eisler, F., 114
Halliday, M. A. K., 28, 30, 38, 80, 97
Hawkins, P., 115, 152
Henderson, D., 6, 96, 99, 113, 126, 127, 150, 156

Hess, R. B., 154, 156
Hymes, D., 10
Irwin, O. C., 10
Isaacs, N., 123
Jones, D., 19, 96, 156
Joos, M., 29
Katz, J. J., 21
Kohlberg, L., 9, 148, 154, *251*
Labov, W. A., 29
Lawton, D., 115
Lovell, K., 148
McIntosh, A., 28, 38, 97
Medawar, P. S., 121
Mohan, B. A., 50n., 80
Morton-Williams, R., 11
Pei, M., 38
Piaget, J., 9, 93–4, 117, 123, 148, *251*
Rackstraw, S. J., 75n., *257*
Raven, J. C., 78
Robinson, W. P., 11, 75n., 115, 126, *257*, *291*
Schatzman, R., 35
Shipman, V. C., 10, 154, 156
Sinclair, A., 39
Skinner, B. F., 71
Strauss, A., 35
Strevens, P., 28, 38, 97
Templin, M. C., 10
Turner, G. J., 50n., 80
Ure, J. N., 28
Vernon, P. E., 11
Vygotsky, L. S., 94
Wechsler, D., 123
Wiseman, S., 11
Young, D., 113, 150, 156
Zipf, G. K., 68

Subject Index

N.B. Page numbers in roman refer to Vol I and those in italic Vol II

accuracy of mothers' answers, 97, 98, 100, 101, 106, 112, 113, 153, 156–7; *see also* truth
adjuncts, 152; in mothers' answers (simplifying), 103, 108, 109, 114, (uninformative), 102, 108, 109, 114
analogy (appeals to), 65, 74, 98, 110,

118, 122, 134, 147, 153, *245*, *290*, *314*, *331*
answers: criteria for separating from non-answers, 23–4; definition, 22–3; description, 25–48; form, 23 (*see* grammar; lexis); length, 276–7; *see also* context; mode, etc.

347

appropriateness, 67, 97, 148, *289, 292*; defined, 25; relationships within, 260; *see also* context of answer; grammar of answer; inappropriateness; lexis of answer; mode of answer

authority (appeals to), 65, 73, 98, 110, 134, 147, 150, 153, 157, *194, 209, 290, 314*; focus of answer mode and, *245, 246, 248–9, 251*; form and context and, *271–2*; modes for non-why questions and, *253, 254*; moral content questions, *211, 217, 221–2, 230, 232, 235, 283, 329–30*; sub-categories, *232, 235*; *see also* cause; consequence; restatement of question

boys: acceptability of answers, *275–6*; game structure answers, 88–9; mothers' answers to, 106–7, 108, 112–13; non-why questions and, *201–4*; variables of sample, 6–7, 77, 129, 130; *see also* sex differences; social class differences

categories: additional groupings, *185*; validity, *184–5, 279*

categorization (appeals to), 66, 74, 98, 110, 118, 122, 134, 135–6, 148, 150, 153, 157, *194–5, 205*, 237, *281, 282–3, 288, 290, 314–15*; cause and, *224–5, 283*; consequence and, *213–16, 217, 223–5, 226–7, 241–2, 283*; focus of answer mode and, *245, 246, 248, 249*; form and context of non-why questions, *269–71, 289*; modes (non-why questions), *252–3, 254, 255, 256*; moral content questions, *213–15, 223–6, 232–4, 235, 279, 331–3*; picture answers, *83–5*, 92; sub-categories, *232–4, 235, 279, 281–2*; *see also* emotions; irrelevance; presupposition; refusal responses; restatement of question

cause (appeals to), 9, 37, 66–7, 74, 97, 98, 104, 110, 118, 153, *195, 199, 205, 209, 238, 281, 290, 315–16, 333*; authority and, *221–2, 228–9, 230, 241, 279, 288*; explanation of 5-year-olds, 79; explanation of 7-year-olds, 122, 134, 148, 150; focus of answer mode and, *246, 247, 248, 249*; form and context and, *272–3*; modes (non-why questions), *253–4*; social content questions, 216, *217, 227–30, 231, 234, 235, 283, 317–18*; sub-categories, *234, 235*; *see also* categorization; consequence; irrelevance; restatement of question

child rearing: linguistic development, 2; social class differences, 10

children, *see* sample

circularity, sympathetic, in mothers' answers, 103–4, 108, 109

closed questions, *see* questions

code, *see* elaborated code; restricted code

coding-frame, 67, 75, 78–80, 82–3, 86–7, *293–340*; mothers' answers, 100–4; non-why questions, 311; validity, *184–5, 231, 280–7, 292*

collocation, 39

communication index, 76, 127; basis, 77–8; categorization and, 83–4; defined, 6; game explanation and, 92; mothers' answers, 104, 105, 113; of sample, 77, 99; picture answers, 92; 'toy elephant' answers, 80, 81, 82

completeness, 67, 97, 148–9, *289, 292*; defined, 25; relationships within, *260–1*; social class and, 80, 81; *see also* context of answer; grammar of answer; incompleteness; lexis of answer; mode of answer

concordant area, 26

consequence (appeals to), 37, 66–7, 74, 96, 97, 104, 108–9, 110, 113, 118, 122, 134, 147–8, 150, 153, 154, 157, *195–6, 209, 281, 290, 316–17, 318*; authority and, *215, 217, 221–2, 226, 230, 279, 283, 288*; categorization and, *213–16, 217, 223–5, 226–7, 241–2, 283*; cause and *218–19, 227–8, 288*; consequence and, *239–40*; focus of answer mode and, *244, 246, 248, 249*; form and context and, *272–3*; modes (non-why questions), *253–4*; moral content questions, *215–16, 226–7, 234, 235, 316–17, 333–5*; sub-categories, 234, 235, 236, (categorization), 242; unique person specification and, *254*; *see* emotion; regularity; restatement of question

content of answers, 23, *187*; prediction, *247–8*

content of questions, 5, 37, 148

context of answers, 24, 26–35, 97, 152–3, *187, 289*; appropriateness, 14, 32–3, 57, 73, 97, *182, 257, 284*; completeness, 14, 33–4, 57, 73, 131, 135, 147, 150, *182, 190, 257, 288, 304–6*, ('when' and 'where' modes), *267*; evaluation of categories, *283–7*; inappropriateness, 54–5, 102, 122, 131, 135, 147, 150, *190, 298–9*; incompleteness, 55, 122, 157, *257*; presupposition, 14, 34–5, 38, 56–8, 72, 97, 131, 147, 152, *182, 256–7, 289*; relationships at level of, *260*; *see* elaborated code; restricted code

contiguity, and 'where' and 'when' questions, *199–200*

control, language as means of, 96, 154

Control and Communication Index, 121, 127, 128–9, 130, 154, *183, 188, 282*; 7-year-olds' answers and, 136, 137–46, 149–50

control group, 7, 126, 149

co-occurrence, 10–11

core area, defined, 26

correlational analysis, 184–5; limitations, 185–7

Crichton Vocabulary Scale, 78

curiosity, 8

developmental social psychology, and research, 7, 9–10

discipline situations, *226, 231*; mothers' behaviour, 116–17, 150, 154; *see also* Control and Communication Index

education: language functions in, 11–12, 96, 116–17, 155–6, 292; relevance of research, 7–9, 156–7

effect explanations, *see* consequence

egocentricity, 9, 93–4

elaborated code, 70–4, 93–5, 97, 98, 99, 292; context of answers, 71–3; disorganization of speech, 112; form of answers, 74; mode of answers, 73–4; system of knowledge, 147; *see* communication index; Speech Complexity Index; Use of Language programme

emotions (appeals to), 65, 98, 104, 110, 113, *194, 196, 209, 281, 290, 314*; categorization and, *212, 213–15, 217, 222–3, 230*; consequence and, *211–13, 215–16, 217, 222, 230*; focus of answer mode and, *245, 247, 248*; moral content questions, *211–13, 217, 222–3, 230, 330*; negative, form and context and, *273–4*

English Picture Vocabulary Test, 76, 78, 126, 127–9, 130

essence (appeals to), 64–5, 73, 98, 110, 122, 134, 147, *245, 248, 290, 313, 328–9*

evasion, in mothers' answers, 97, 98, 100, 105, 112, 117, 153

finishers, redundant, in mothers' answers, 103, 108, 109, 114

form (answers), *see* grammar; lexis

formality, 28, 29, 31–2, 72

functional definition, *269, 281, 310*; related to 'why' mode, *252, 254–5*

game: choice, 85–6; explanation, 76, 85–92, 152; players, 86, 87, 152; results, 88–92; scoring, 86–7; structure, 86–7

generality, *see* universality

girls: non-why questions and, 201–4, 288; variables of sample, 6–7, 77, 127–9; *see also* sex differences; social class differences

grammar of answers, 38–9, 152–3, *289*; appropriateness, 14, 40–2, 56, 74, 76, 97, *257, 284*; completeness, 14, 43–4, 57, 74, 79, *182, 257, 284*; correlated with authority, *271–2*; evaluation of categories, *283–7*; inappropriateness, 51, 102, 122, 134, 151, 157, *189, 190, 256–7, 284–6, 295–6*, 297–8, ('when' and 'where' modes), *266–7*; incompleteness, 52, 122, 134, 136, 151, 157, *190, 284–6, 299–301*; mistakes in, *190, 286, 288*, 297–8; presupposition, 14, 45–7, 52–3, 57, 64, 74, 122, 134, 148–9, *182, 186, 191, 257, 284, 289, 306–7*, (categorization) *269–71*, ('when' and 'where' modes), *270–1*; relationships at level of, *258–9*; *see also* elaborated code; restricted code

grammar of questions, 3–5

Hall-Jones social class scale, 77

'how' questions, 2n., 4–5, 123, 124; modes, 4, 5, 20, 36, 37; modes of answer, 60–1, *198*; *see also* game; non-why questions; 'toy elephant'

inappropriateness: categorization and, *269–70, 287*; coding-frame, *295–9, 326, 338–9*; functional definition, *269*; incompleteness and, *263*; relationships within, *260, 261, 264–5*; 'when' and 'where' modes, *266–7, 271, 284*; *see also* appropriateness; context of answer; grammar of answer; lexis of answer; mode of answer

incompleteness: coding - frame, *299–306*; functional definition, *269*; non-aspect items and, *263*; relationships within, *260–1, 264–5*; 'when' and 'where' modes and, *267–8*; *see also* completeness; context of answer; grammar of answer; inappropriateness; lexis of answer; mode of answer

indefinites, in mothers' answers, 102, 108, 109, 113
inequality, appeals to, *336*
information in mothers' answers, 96, 97, 98, 100, 101–2, 106–8, 112, 113, 117–18, 153
instruction, language as medium of, 96, 116–17
Intelligence Test scores, 121, *183*, *188*, *282*; categories, 78; game structure answers and, 88–9, 92; mothers' answers and, 104, 105, 107, 110–11, 112–13; picture answers and, 83–4, 92; role differentiation and, 91; of sample, 6, 76–7, 99, 126; 7-year-olds' answers and, 136, 137–46, 149–50; 'toy elephant' answers and, 80, 81, 92
intonation, 3, 33, 158
irrelevance, *205*, *319*; categorization and, *240*; cause and, *228;* regularity and, *210*, *211*

knowledge, hierarchical system of, 118, 120, 122, 147, 150

language: functions, 11–12, 70, 96, 116–18, (referential), 155; *see also* elaborated code; restricted code
learning: language functions, 11–12, 96, 116–17, 155–6, *292;* relevance of research, 7–9, 156–7
lexical continuity, 23, 24, 39, 147
lexical set, 39
lexis of answers, 4, 97, 152–3, *289;* appropriateness, 14, 42–3, 57, 74, 76, 97, *182*, *257*, *284*; authority and, *271–2;* completeness, 14, 34, 44–5, 57, 74, 79, *182*, *257*; evaluation of categories, *283–7;* inappropriateness, 51, 122, 134, 151, *189–90*, *298*, (categorization) *269–70*, *289*, ('when' and 'where' modes), 271; incompleteness, 52, 97, 102, 122, 134, 136, 151, 152, 157, *190*, *257*, *284–6*, *287*, *301–4*, ('when' and 'where' modes), *267–8;* presupposition, 14, 47, 53–4, 58, 64, 74, 148–9, *182*, *186*, *191*, *257*, *289*, *307–8;* relationships at level of, *259–60; see also* elaborated code; restricted code
linguistic inconsistency, *see* role differentiation
linguistic structure: children's answers, 50, 52–3, 80, 82, 92: mothers' answers, 97–8, 100, 102–4, 108, 112
linguistics: aims and methods, *181–3;* data collection, *182;* relevance of research, 7, 9

middle class: mothers' answers to 'wh' questions, 2, 96–118 *passim; see also* elaborated code; social class
minimizers in mothers' answers, 103, 108, 109
mirror images in mothers' answers, 103, 109, 113
mode of answers, 35–8, 97, 122, 135–6, 152–3, *182–3;* appropriateness, 14, 36–7; choice, 14; coding, 67, 104, *311–40;* completeness, 14, 37–8, *198;* content of question and, *5*, 37; foci, *244–51;* higher order groupings, *244–51*, *279*, *287–9;* inappropriateness, 79, 122; presupposition, 14, 38; social class and, 81, 122, 131, 134, 147–9, 153, *205;* validity (separations), *281–3*, *289–90*, (sub-categories) *205–36*, *281–2*, *290*, (summed modes) *236–43; see also* elaborated codes; restricted codes
mode of questions, 5
moral judgment, 9
moral questions, *see* 'why' questions, moral matters
mothers: answers to 'wh' questions, 2, 96–118, 152–3, 158–63, (validity) 115–16

'noisy' items in mothers' answers, 98, 112, 157
non-answers, 23, 24
non-questions, 21
non-why questions: answer mode (evaluation of separation), *201–3*, *281*, (examination) *199–204*, *251–6*, (exclusiveness) *198*, (scoring) *198*, *311;* formal and contextual features of answers, *256–65;* higher order groupings, *203–4*, *287;* relationships (levels and aspects of answers), *261–2*, (modes, form and context) *266–9;* variables of matrix, *189–93*

objective reference system, 73, 93–4, 148, 150
oddity, denial of, 63, 73, 98, 122, 134, 147, *244*, *290*, *313*, *326*
omissions, from mothers' answers, 102, 109
open-ended questions, *see* questions
overcompleteness, 33–4, 56
overgeneralization, 101, 102, 113

participants: formality between, 28, 31–2; question/answer exchange, 27, 30–1
particularization, 84–5, 86, 87, 89–90, 92, 93
personal reference system, 73, 93

phrases, inessential in mothers' answers, 103, 108, 109, 113, 114
pictures, 76, 82–5, 92–3
prepositions, *192, 257, 263, 309*
presupposition, 14, 67, 76, 97, 122, 150, 157, *284, 292*; categorization and, *269–71*; coding-frame, *306–8*; defined, 25; relationships within, 261; 'when' and 'where' modes, *268, 270–1*; *see also* context of answer; grammar of answer; lexis of answer; mode of answer
principle explanations, 78–9, 81, 92, *198*
probing of answers, 120, 122, 124–6, 147, *199, 215, 321, 325*
process explanations, 78–9, 81, *198*
pronouns, used instead of nouns, 97, 134, 152, *302*
purpose (appeals to) in mothers' answers, 113

questioning: functions, 15–16; prerequisites, 16–17, 155; scope, 21
questions: closed, 3–4, 17–18, 19, 122; content, 5, 37, 148; context, 6, 148; difficulty, 5; 5-year-olds, 75–6; forms, 3–5, 18–20; higher order grouping, 5; modes, 5; mothers, 99–100, 158–63; open-ended, 4–5, 17–18, 19–21, 123, (categories) 19–21; 7-year-olds, 122–5, 163–71; types of, 17–18; *see also* restatement of question

refusal responses, *197, 205*; categorization and, *223, 224*; *see also* regularity
register, 27–8; scales, 28–32, 71, 72, 148
regularity (appeals to), 64, 73, 98, 110, 113, 117, 122, 134, 147, 150, 153, 157, *194, 199, 209, 313, 328*; consequence and, *219, 220, 227*; focus of answer mode and, *245, 246, 248–9*; modes (non-why questions), *254*; physical content questions and, *210–11, 217, 219–21, 230, 234–5*; refusal responses and, *219, 221, 230*; sub-categories, *232; 234–5, 282, 328*; *see also* restatement of question
relevance, network of ('when' and 'where' questions), *200, 290*
replacement group, 40, 42, 44, 45, 46, 52, 53, 56, 57, 62, 74
research: outline, 1–12; pitfalls, 119–21, 146–7; reasons, 7–12
residual area, 26
restatement of question, 63–4, 73, 98, 110, 117, 122, 150, 153, 157, *194, 290, 313, 327–8*; authority and, *221–2*; categorization and, *225–6*; cause and, *228–9, 230*; consequence and, *226, 283*; focus of answer mode and, *244, 246–7, 248*; regularity and, *219*
restricted code, 11–12, 70–4, 93–5, 97, 98, 99, *292*; consequences, 155–6, *292*; context of answers, 71–3; disorganization of speech, 112; form of answers, 74; mode of answers, 73–4; mothers' answers, 108, 114; sociological conditions, 155–7; *see also* communication index; Use of Language programme
role: differentiation, 87–8, 91–2, 93; scale of register, 28, 29, 31, 72; specification, 5, 50, 55, 97, 117, *200–1, 252, 290*

sample (mothers), 6, 96, 99, (children) 6–7, 77, 127–9, 130
scoring procedure, *see* coding-frame
self-reference, 73, 93, 94
sex differences: aspects of answers, *260–1*; categorization and, *282–3*; game explanation and, 92; grammar of answers (non-why questions), *258–9, 284*; length of answers, 276–7; lexis of answers (non-why questions), *259–60, 284*; modes (non-why and 'why' questions), *255–6*; mothers' answers, 104, 105, 106–7, 112–13; picture answers, 83–4, 92; 'toy elephant' answers, 81; validity of mode separations (non-why questions), *201–2*, ('why' questions) *210–43 passim*; 'why' modes and form and context, *274–5*; *see* boys; girls
social class, *183, 188*; attitudes to 'wh' questions, 117–18; contextual presupposition, 35, 131, 147, 152; discipline situations, 116–17; game structure answers, 88–9, 92; index, 77; linguistic development, 2, 10–11, 94–5; mothers' answers (information), 104, 105, 106–8, 117–18, 152–3, (linguistic context) 108, 112, 152–3, (mode) 108–11, 113, 153, (predicted differences), 98, 112, (validity) 115–16; neighbourhood peers, 122, 127, 130, 136, 137, 149; organized knowledge, 120, 147; particularization, 84–5, 89–90, 92, 93; picture answers, 84, 85, 92; regularity, *282*; 7-year-old boys' answers, 129, 135–6, 146–151; 7-year-old girls' answers, 129, 131–51 *passim*; social psycho-

logical characteristics, 76, 98, 112, 155; substitution, 122, 146, 148–9; 'toy elephant' answers, 80, 81–2, 92; Use of Language Programme and, 132–3, 135; *see also* middle class; role differentiation; truth; universality; working class

socialization, relevance of research, 7–9, 96, 155–7

sociocentricity, 9, 93–4

socio-linguistics, 6, 7, 10–11, 148, 290, 291

sociological conditions, restricted code and, 155–7

speech: egocentric, 9, 93–4; socio-centric, 9, 93–4

Speech Complexity Index, 126, 132–3, 135, 149

substitution, 42, 47, 51, 53, 57, 58, 67–8, 122, 146, 148–9, *191, 258, 264, 284, 289, 302–3;* coding-frame, *308–9;* in mothers' answers, 102, 108, 109, 112, 114; relationships within, *261;* 'when' and 'where' modes, *268*

'toy elephant': questions, 76; results, 81–2, 92; scoring, 78–80

Trotin pictures, *see* pictures

truth, 92; scoring, 80; social class, 80, 81, 106; *see also* accuracy of mothers' answers

uncertainty in mothers' answers, 103, 109, 113

unique person specification, 50, *252, 254, 269, 281*

universality, 84–5, 86, 87, 92, 93, 101, 114

Use of Language Programme, 7, 121, 122, 126; social class of girls and, 132–3, 135, 149

vagueness, 14, 45, 52, *190–1, 263, 267, 268, 272–3, 286, 288, 301–3;* in mothers' answers, 97, 102, 108, 109, 113, 114

values and attitudes, 155, 156

'wh' questions, 2, 9; alternation and, 10; Bernstein's theory, 152–7; defined, 2n.; 5-year-old children and, 75–95; restricted code users and, 70–1; 7-year-old children and, 119–51; social class, 117–18; vagueness, 14; *see also* questions, types of; *and types of questions*

'what' questions, 4–5, 19, 20–1, 123, 124; mode of answer, 67–9, *193, 198, 199; see* non-why questions

'when' questions, 4–5, 19, 20–1, 123, 124; modes of answer, 59–60, 73, 122, 131–3, 147–8, 150, 157, *192–3, 198, 199–204, 251–6, 281, 287, 289–90, 311,* (form and context) *266–9,* (predisposing factors) *199–200,* ('why' mode) *252–4; see also* non-why questions

'where' questions, 4–5, 19, 123, 124–5; modes of answer, 58–9, 73, 122, 131–3, 147–8, 150, 157, *192–3, 198, 199–204, 281, 287, 289–90, 311,* (form and context and) *266–9,* (non-aspect items and) *264,* (predisposing factors) *199–200,* ('why' mode) *252–4;* mothers' answers, 96; *see also* non-why questions

'which' questions, 4–5, 19, 20–1, 123; mode of answer, 67–8; *see also* non-why questions

'who' questions, 4–5, 19, 123, 124; context of answers, 54–8; form of answers, 50–4, 97; mode of answer, 50, *193, 198, 199, 281, 289–90, 311,* (predisposing factors) *200–1,* ('why' mode) *252, 254;* mothers' answers, 96; *see also* non-why questions; unique person specification

'why' questions, 19, 122, 123–5; modes of answers, 62–7, 108–10, 134, 147, *193–6, 198, 199, 205–51, 279,* (coding-frame) *312–40,* (evaluation of coding) *281–3, 290,* (higher order groupings) *244–51, 279, 287–9,* (non-why modes) *251–6,* (validity) *205–36, 236–43, 281–2, 290;* moral matters, 5, 73, 118, 123, 124–5, 134, 148, 150, *188, 194–6, 199, 209, 288,* (coding-frame) *320–42 (see also* authority; categorization; consequence; emotions); mothers' answers, 96, 104–118 *passim,* 123; physical matters, 5, 118, 123, 124, 134, 148, 150, *194, 195, 199, 205, 209, 279, 288, 315–16 (see* regularity); probing of answers, 120, 122, 124–6, 147, *199, 215, 321, 325;* restricted code users and, 73, 104–18 *passim;* social matters, 5, 73, 118, 123, 124, *195, 196, 199, 205, 209, 317–18,* (cause and) *216, 217, 227–30, 231, 234, 235, 283, 317–18;* subject matter, 5, 123, 148, *199*

wishes (appeals to), 65, *314, 330*

words, number of, in mothers' answers, 101, 107–8, 112

working class: linguistic development, 94–5; mothers' answers to 'wh' questions, 2, 96–118 *passim;* under-achievement of, 11, *292; see also* restricted code; social class